WARRIOR • 159

US MACV-SOG RECONNAISSANCE TEAM IN VIETNAM

GORDON L ROTTMAN

ILLUSTRATED BY BRIAN DELF

Series editor Marcus Cowper

OSPREY PUBLISHING
Bloomsbury Publishing Plc

Kemp House, Chawley Park, Cumnor Hill, Oxford OX2 9PH, UK
29 Earlsfort Terrace, Dublin 2, Ireland
1385 Broadway, 5th Floor, New York, NY 10018, USA
Email: info@ospreypublishing.com
www.ospreypublishing.com

OSPREY is a trademark of Osprey Publishing Ltd

First published in Great Britain in 2011
Transferred to digital print in 2015

A catalog record for this book is available from the British Library.

Print ISBN: 978 1 84908 513 7
ePDF: 978 1 84908 514 4
ePub: 978 1 84908 942 5

Editorial by Ilios Publishing Ltd, Oxford, UK – www.iliospublishing.com
Page layout by Mark Holt
Index by Alison Worthington
Typeset in Sabon and Myriad Pro
Originated by PDQ Media
Printed and bound in India by Replika Press Private Ltd.

www.ospreypublishing.com
To find out more about our authors and books visit our website. Here you
will find extracts, author interviews, details of forthcoming events and
the option to sign-up for our newsletter.

Acknowledgments
The author is indebted to Frank Greco (CCC), Bruce Perry (CCS), John L.
Plaster (CCN), A. J. Sharp (CCS), Trey Moore of Moore Militaria, and Steve
Sherman of RADIX Press for their invaluable assistance.

Artist's note
Readers may care to note that the original paintings from which
the color plates in this book were prepared are available for private sale.
All reproduction copyright whatsoever is retained by the Publishers.
All enquiries should be addressed to:

Brian Delf,
7 Burcot Park,
Burcot,
Abingdon,
OX14 3DH
United Kingdom

The Publishers regret that they can enter into no correspondence upon
this matter.

Measurement conversions
Imperial measurements are used almost exclusively throughout this
book. The exception is weapon calibers, which are given in their official
designation, whether metric or imperial. The following data will help in
converting the imperial measurements to metric.

1 mile = 1.6km
1lb = 0.45kg
1oz = 28g
1 yard = 0.9m
1ft = 0.3m
1in. = 2.54cm/25.4mm
1 gal = 4.5 liters
1pt = 0.47 liters
1 ton (US) = 0.9 tonnes
1hp = 0.745kW

Abbreviations

AIT	Advanced Individual Training
AO	area of operations
BCT	Basic Combat Training
CCN, CCC, CCS	Command and Control North, Central, and South
CIA	Central Intelligence Agency
CIDG	Civilian Irregular Defense Group
CO	commanding officer
CS	tear gas
FAC	forward air controller
FOB	forward operations base
IAD	immediate-action drill
LZ	landing zone
MACV–SOG	Military Assistance Command, Vietnam – Studies and Observation Group
MOS	military occupation specialty
NCO	noncommissioned officer
NVA	North Vietnamese Army
O&I	operations and intelligence
PZ	pick-up zone
RON	remain overnight
RT	reconnaissance team
SFGA	Special Force Group (Airborne)
SITREP	situation report
SLAM	Search, Location, and Annihilation Mission company
SOI	signal operating instructions
SOP	standard operating procedures
USSF	United States Special Forces
VC	Viet Cong
WP	white phosphorus ("Willie Pete")

CONTENTS

MACV-SOG RECONNAISSANCE TEAM IN VIETNAM

INTRODUCTION

Throughout the 1960s the insurgency in South Vietnam gradually escalated. While denying involvement, North Vietnam had long supported the insurgency with arms, munitions, supplies, and advisers. Some small North Vietnamese Army (NVA) units were operating in South Vietnam in support of the Viet Cong (VC), the military arm of the National Liberation Front, the outlawed South Vietnamese communist party.

While some of the troops and materials arrived in the south by crossing the demilitarized zone along the 17th Parallel, which separated North and South Vietnam, and others by boat, by far the most were sent through Laos and Cambodia. This was accomplished via the infamous Ho Chi Minh Trail, which North Vietnam had begun to develop in mid-1959. The North Vietnamese government issued a resolution changing its "political struggle" in the south to an "armed struggle." At the end of 1964 the first NVA regiment marched down the Ho Chi Minh Trail and entered South Vietnam. Events escalated rapidly. In February 1965 the US authorized air attacks against North Vietnam. In March the first US Marine ground-combat troops arrived and the following month US troops were authorized to conduct offensive operations. In May the first US Army conventional ground-combat troops arrived and NVA divisions began deploying via the Ho Chi Minh Trail.

Known as the Truong Son Road after the 1,500–8,000ft Laotian mountain range it traversed, the name "Ho Chi Minh Trail" was bestowed by the Americans, and was later adopted by the North Vietnamese. It was not merely a trail or road winding through the forested hills and valleys of Laos and Cambodia; the route was a network of interconnected roads and foot trails allowing alternate ways to bypass flooding and deceive air attacks. It was never known what roads would be in use or which were under repair at any one time, misleading analysts. The trailhead was at Techepone, inside southeastern Laos. Truck convoys reached it over numerous roads running out of North Vietnam. The trucks were for supplies; troop units and replacements traveled on foot. Units traveled south in battalion- and company-sized increments and transported their own crew-served weapons. Replacements traveled in groups varying in size from five men to up to 500, the most common being 40–50. They carried only individual weapons and five days' supply of rice. They would march for four or five days, staying at a way station each night, after which they would have a rest day and were resupplied with rations.

This short section of the Ho Chi Minh Trail in Laos was a highly desirable target because it snaked along a hillside above a river. B-52 bombs bursting on either side would bury or collapse the road. Approaching insertion helicopters could discern the Trail's route from miles away. (John Plaster)

Huge amounts of supplies were shipped south. In order to supplement the trucks, ox carts, reinforced bicycles, and even elephants were used. Supplies also flowed down the region's rivers, allowing some to get through during the wet season, which essentially shut down the roads. Even fuel pipelines were laid. The foot and bicycle trails were 2–5ft wide, while truck roads were 18ft wide. In 1964, 20–30 tons of supplies a day were hauled down the trail. By the 1965 dry season it was 90 tons a day.

It developed into a monumental logistics effort, operated by the 559th Transportation Group, which maintained the trail system, supply caches, storage dumps, barracks, maintenance facilities, hospitals, and command-and-control facilities, as well as base areas where the supplies and troops were marshaled and sent into South Vietnam on branch trails. The 559th Transportation Group was organized into 15 logistical-base units (*binh tram*), later 27, each responsible for 30–50 miles of trail. They typically were composed of two truck-transport, engineer, and air-defense battalions and single communications-liaison, signal, security, and medical battalions. Sometimes there was an SA-2 missile battalion and a food-production unit, which cultivated gardens and raised livestock. Besides defending, repairing, maintaining, and expanding the trail system, the base units operated way stations and provided guides. Local Laotian and Cambodian guides were employed until 1965, after which only VC/NVA communications-liaison agents were used, for security purposes. The 559th's motto was "Build roads to advance, fight the enemy to travel."

A GAZ-51 cargo truck runs down the muddy Ho Chi Minh Trail as it is photographed by an SOG RT. In many places the Trail was wide enough for two-way traffic. (John Plaster)

The weather played a major role in both the NVA's supply effort and Free World measures to interdict it. The southwest monsoon (rainy season) ran from mid-May to mid-September, bringing heavy rains, overcast skies, and high temperatures. The northwest monsoon (dry season) lasted from mid-October to mid-March, with limited rain and moderate temperatures. This is when the Trail saw its heaviest use, and when American reconnaissance and air interdiction aimed at it was at its most intense.

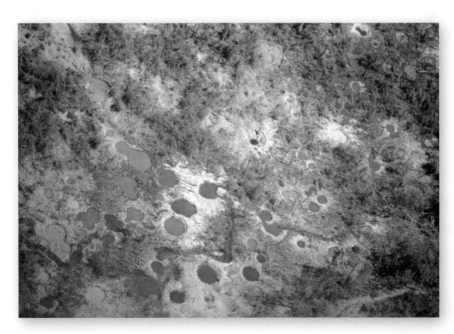

A heavily bomb-blasted portion of the Ho Chi Minh Trail is pockmarked with 500lb, 750lb, and 1,000lb bomb craters. (John Plaster)

Obviously the Ho Chi Minh Trail's use as a logistics and replacement transportation system, its base areas, and the privileged sanctuary it provided the NVA/VC was an extremely important aspect of the Vietnam War. A basic precept of war is to interdict the enemy's line of communications. This was much easier said than done with the Ho Chi Minh Trail. The vast majority of it ran beneath jungle canopy, bridges and fords were camouflaged, and routes were frequently changed. Areas were laid bare by bombs and the spraying of defoliant, but these areas were often bypassed and camouflage screens were erected. Antiaircraft defenses were heavy, and in particularly dangerous areas truck travel was undertaken at night.

A simple dirt road is not as easily disrupted as a modern hard-surfaced highway. A wide highway is easily located, even in forested areas, is straighter than a narrow dirt road snaking beneath the trees, and is easier to hit with a bomb for these reasons. Three things happen when a 750lb general-purpose bomb is dropped on a dirt road: a large hole is created, nearby vegetation is blown away from the hole, and loose soil is displaced and scattered about. Only two things needed to be done to bypass a large hole in a road; nearby vegetation needed to be removed and loose soil laid to provide a new road surface bypassing the hole. The bomb craters also provided water reservoirs and bathing facilities.

The Trail was well protected by air defenses and ground troops. These may not have always been trained infantry and security units, although combat units passing through the area would often be pressed into security and pursuit

A Laotian valley peppered with bomb craters, completely obliterating a portion of the Ho Chi Minh Trail. In some instances the NVA were able to rebuild such a battered section by winding the route through the craters and making it look like it did not exist. In other instances they completely bypassed the area with a new road. (Frank Greco via John Plaster)

An aerial photograph of the Ho Chi Minh Trail showing bulldozer tracks in Laos where overnight repairs of bomb craters have been made. Bulldozer tracks were sometimes confused with tank tracks. Regardless, air attacks on the area to destroy dozers were valuable, as they inhibited efforts to repair the Trail. (Ted Wicorek via John Plaster)

A One-Zero armed with a silencer-equipped .45-cal. M3 "grease gun." A Claymore bag is carried at his right hip and a strobe-light case is on the right shoulder strap of his STABO harness. The man in the background is armed with a 5.56mm XM177E2 submachine gun. (John Plaster)

duties. Service troops would be turned out to search for American reconnaissance teams. There were also very efficient NVA counter-reconnaissance companies who actively sought and pursued recon teams. In order to determine the exact location of the hidden routes, bridges, fords, dumps, rest areas, truck parks, and air defenses, and to determine which trails and roads were in use, the traffic pattern and schedule, etc., someone had to go in on the ground and look at it up close. Aerial visual reconnaissance, aerial photographs, satellite surveillance, and radio interception provided little if any of this much-needed intelligence information.

Prior to 1965 there was no existing unit capable of covertly operating in such a dangerous environment.

MACV–SOG

As with any new and unprecedented initiative, the early days of MACV-SOG were flawed with misconceptions, over-expectation, and mistakes. Aware of extensive NVA infiltration of advisers and supplies, in 1961 the new Kennedy administration implemented a National Security Action Memorandum that expanded the Central Intelligence Agency's authority to introduce South Vietnamese agents into North Vietnam and Laos. The CIA did not have the specialized tactical expertise or the logistical resources to conduct such operations. Army Special Forces and Navy SEALs provided the training expertise. Efforts were made to drop South Vietnamese agents into the North and it proved a disaster. Of the 22 teams inserted in 1961–63, by late 1963

RECON TEAM DUTY POSITIONS	
12-man team	**Six-man team**
1-0 team leader	1-0 team leader
1-1 assistant team leader	1-1 assistant team leader/radio operator
1-2 radio operator	1-2 radio operator (optional)
0-1 indigenous team leader	0-1 indigenous team leader
0-2 interpreter	0-2 interpreter
0-3 grenadier	0-3 grenadier
0-4 grenadier	0-4 scout
0-5 scout	
0-6 scout	
0-7 scout	
0-8 scout	
0-9 scout	
Note: Positions beginning with "1-" were filled by Americans, and those beginning with "0-" were filled by indigenous soldiers.	

In 1969 Project Ford Frum saw SOG members aboard Army O-1 Bird Dog observation aircraft of the 219th Aviation Company photographing points of interest in Laos and Cambodia. Here six NVA graves were revealed in a bomb-shattered bamboo thicket. (Frank Greco via John Plaster)

only four remained operational with most having been killed, captured, or turned. The CIA's ineffective ability to run this program led to many of the paramilitary projects in Vietnam being transferred to the military. Operation *Switchback* in November 1963 turned the programs over to US Special Forces (USSF). This included ground-reconnaissance operations in Laos. The operation was not concluded until December, and Military Assistance Command, Vietnam – Studies and Observation Group (MACV-SOG, pronounced "Mac-Vee-Sogg") was established on January 24, 1964.

The group's cover mission was to conduct analysis of lessons learned in combat involving all branches of service. It was actually a joint unconventional task force tasked with conducting covert strategic reconnaissance missions into Laos and South Vietnam, as well as sabotage and "black" psychological operations. Ground, air, and naval assets were employed to insert, collect, extract, and otherwise support these operations.

MACV–SOG was first headquartered in Cholon outside Saigon, and moved into Saigon in 1966. Its air assets – Air Studies Group – operated infiltration and various specialized support aircraft, both fixed-wing and rotary-wing. The naval assets – Maritime Studies Group – operated specialized high-speed watercraft for infiltration and raiding. The MACV–SOG Training Center and Airborne Operations Group provided specialized training. A Psychological Studies Group operated broadcasting stations. The largest and most important SOG unit was the Ground Studies Group (OP-35). It operated several forward operating bases (FOBs) throughout South Vietnam. These were launch sites for small reconnaissance teams that conducted extremely dangerous intelligence-collection missions, mainly aimed at the Ho Chi Minh Trail. These usually had two or three Americans, with the rest of the team made up of men indigenous to the region. Most of these men were Montagnards, Cambodians, or Nùngs. The SOG began missions into Cambodia in June 1967.

MACV–SOG was assigned some 2,000 Americans, mostly Army Special Forces, and over 8,000 specially selected, highly trained Vietnamese troops of the Special Commando Unit. In all 4,000 USSF troops served in MACV–SOG, along with another 2,700 Army, Air Force, Navy, and Marine personnel, in addition to civilian staff. It had its own air force, composed of US Air Force, South Vietnamese, and Nationalist Chinese helicopter and transport units. On 1 November 1967 MACV–SOG reorganized its ground reconnaissance elements into three field commands: Command and Control North, Central, and South (CCN, CCC, and CCS). SOG, unlike the Ground Studies Group, was a Special Forces unit, even if a high percentage of those in the Ground Studies Group were from the Special Forces. Special Forces soldiers were considered the best recon men because of their flexibility and since they were trained to operate deep within enemy territory and organize guerrillas. This new mission would also take place behind enemy lines and would demand flexibility and adaptability.

MACV–SOG had five primary responsibilities. These were:
1. Cross-border operations conducted to disrupt the VC, Khmer Rouge, Pathet Lao, and NVA in their own territories.
2. Keeping track of all imprisoned and missing Americans and conducting rescue operations (Bright Light).
3. Training and dispatching agents into North Vietnam to run resistance movements and intelligence-collection operations.
4. "Black" psychological operations, such as establishing false NVA broadcasting stations inside North Vietnam.
5. "Gray" psychological operations.

This Soviet- or Chinese-made 2½-ton GAZ-51 cargo truck was halted and the driver snatched by a CCC RT. A yet-to-be-ignited AN-M14 thermite grenade sits on the hood. North Vietnam lost thousands of trucks on the Trail, mainly to US air attacks based on SOG intelligence. (John Plaster)

MACV–SOG was also entrusted with specific tasks, such as apprehending and killing selected enemy personnel and the recovery of sensitive documents and equipment if it was lost or captured by the enemy.

CCN, CCC, and CCS conducted covert cross-border reconnaissance missions into Laos and Cambodia and some operations inside South Vietnam. They each consisted of a reconnaissance company composed of a varied number of reconnaissance teams (RTs), and "Hatchet" reaction forces operating as exploitation platoons and companies. It is the RTs that are best known and that undertook the most dangerous missions.

These extremely perilous missions were oriented around collecting intelligence on NVA traffic, operations, and activities, as well as facilities (rest camps, supply transfer points, truck marshalling areas, supply depots, antiaircraft-gun positions, bridges, fuel dumps, pipelines, etc.) found along the Ho Chi Minh Trail.

Besides collecting intelligence, they undertook sabotage missions, tapped telephone lines, planted electronic sensors, apprehended prisoners for interrogation, inserted exploding ammunition into dumps, conducted bomb-damage assessment (BDA), and searched for downed airmen. The intelligence collected on these missions supported the extensive aerial interdiction campaign conducted by the US Air Force on the Trail. While the RTs attempted to avoid contact with the enemy, they would fight back viciously if compromised. The Presidential Unit Citation awarded to MACV–SOG best describes this: "Pursued by human trackers and even bloodhounds, these small teams outmaneuvered, outfought, and outran their numerically superior foe."

There was a high chance of being detected and engaged in enemy territory. Extraction took considerable time, and, by the time helicopters arrived, an RT's location and situation had often changed drastically. They could not be supported by artillery when operating inside Laos and Cambodia. Fighter-bombers could support RTs in Laos, but not in Cambodia, as this was forbidden by Washington. Helicopter gunships could support RTs in both

The preferred means of extraction was simply for the chopper to sit down on the ground and for the RT to pile into the bird. It was by far the fastest means of boarding the extraction helicopter. It was also safer and more comfortable than "string" (STABO harness) or ladder extractions. (Mike Sloniker via John Plaster)

countries. The US officially had no troops deployed in these supposedly neutral countries. While those countries' governments may have declared themselves neutral, the reality was that the NVA/VC operated freely in these privileged sanctuaries, maintaining huge base areas, logistical facilities, and lines of communication. The SOG RTs were some of the few Free World units habitually operating beyond the artillery umbrella.

RECRUITMENT AND SELECTION

The USSF soldiers in MACV–SOG had a wide variety of experience prior to volunteering for the Special Forces. Young NCOs with at least one enlistment (three years' service) under their belt were most desired. The Special Forces were intended to train guerrillas, counterinsurgency troops, and other countries' special-operations units, and they needed a degree of experience to do this. The need for Special Forces troops became acute in 1966, and it was opened up to soldiers still in their first tour of duty. They were still required to meet all other Special Forces standards. That meant that they had to have

A UH-1H Huey extracts an RT during training using STABO rigs. This was a harness arrangement incorporated into the recon man's web gear in lieu of load-bearing equipment suspenders. A Special Forces NCO and two officers developed the system in 1969 at the MACV Recondo School. (Dale Boswell via John Plaster)

a General Technical (GT) score of 100, the same as required for officers, have a high-school diploma, and be at least 20 years of age. The GT was a form of IQ test. They had to pass the Army Physical Fitness Test (APFT) to airborne standards, the Combat Water Survival Test (CWST), and the Special Forces Selection Battery. The latter was a series of tests of personality, critical-decision-making ability, self-location skills (using a series of photos), and Morse-code aptitude. They also had to have a clean police record and be qualified for a Top Secret security clearance. They were required to be triple volunteers; that is, they must have volunteered for the Army, airborne, and Special Forces. Qualified conscripts were accepted, but they had to extend their two year enlistment period to three years. Upon completion of Special Forces training, which generally took 6–12 months, they were required to have at least 18 months remaining in their enlistment. If not, they had to extend it by at least a year.

First-enlistment volunteers were recruited during basic training or when attending jump school. Many Special Forces volunteers had served in the 82nd or 101st Airborne Divisions or other airborne units. Still others may have served in any type of unit, including service support. Their diversity of skills was considered valuable. The challenge at this point was getting the approval of their first sergeant, sergeant major, and commanding officer, who were generally reluctant to lose a good man.

Four recon men are extracted on "strings," that is, by STABO extraction. The canvas panels were an effort to reduce the spinning effect caused by the helicopter's rotor downwash. (John Plaster)

All US Army soldiers undertook the eight-week Basic Combat Training (BCT) course. They then undertook Advanced Individual Training (AIT) at training centers or at branch service schools for the more technical skills. Most of these courses lasted 8–12 weeks. Upon completion the soldier was awarded a Military Occupation Specialty (MOS) identifier. Light infantrymen, for example, were assigned the MOS "11B" after eight weeks' training[1]. This was the preferred MOS for Special Forces volunteers who were selected during BCT. It was a critical MOS because of the demands for light infantrymen brought on by the Vietnam War, and if slots were unavailable many future Special Forces soldiers were sent to combat-engineer (12B) training at Fort Belvoir, Virginia. The eight-week 12B training was considered as valuable to Special Forces troops as that for 11B. They were taught many of the combat and patrolling skills of infantrymen, as well as demolitions, the use of booby traps and mines, fortification, and obstacle construction, amongst other skills.

Before attending Special Forces training volunteers went through the Airborne School at Fort Benning, Georgia. Commonly called "jump school," it was three weeks long and physically intense. Typically, around 30 percent of a class washed out. Five jumps were required for award of the coveted jump wings.[2]

1 Infantry training (BCT and AIT) is discussed in Warrior 98: *US Army Infantryman in Vietnam 1965–73*.
2 This is discussed in detail in Warrior 132: *US Army Long-Range Patrol Scout in Vietnam 1965–71*.

SFC Jerry "Mad Dog" Shriver of CCS is armed with a .45-cal. M3 "grease gun" fitted with a silencer. The silencer could not be fitted to the M3A1. An M26 fragmentation grenade is on his right harness strap and a Gerber Mk II fighting knife is on his left harness strap. (Jim Fleming via John Plaster)

Special Forces training was conducted at the John F. Kennedy Center for Special Warfare (Airborne) at Fort Bragg, North Carolina[3]. Assigned to the Special Forces Training Group (SFTG), students found training to be different from anything they had previously experienced. They were there to learn and it was very much an academic environment. The harassment they had previously experienced in BCT, AIT, and jump school was virtually absent, unless one earned it.

Phase I of Special Forces Tactics and Techniques was four weeks of land navigation, basic survival, patrolling, and methods of instruction. It was here that the Special Forces student found that training others was his primary job. They were awarded the green beret at the end of this phase.

There was a break of several weeks between each training phase, during which students performed work details, kitchen police (KP) duty, and acted as counter-guerrilla (CG) forces. In the latter they acted as the aggressors against the students undertaking their field-training exercises, which lasted one week for Phases I and II, and two weeks for Phase III. Serving as a CG proved to be a valuable part of the men's training, providing them with more patrolling, land-navigation, and tactical experience. The Phase I field-training exercises saw many wash out, as it was demanding in land-navigation techniques, evasion skills, and physical endurance.

Recruits then received their Special Forces MOS training in Phase II. These specializations included Engineer (12B, ten weeks), Light and Heavy Weapons (11B and 11C, eight weeks), Operations and Intelligence (O&I)

3 Special Forces training is described in Warrior 28: *Green Beret in Vietnam 1957–73.*

(11F, 12 weeks), Communications (05B, 16 weeks), and Medical (91C, 32 weeks). These jobs were identified by the same MOS codes as their conventional equivalents, but they were very different and more in-depth. An "S" special skill identifier was added to their MOS (e.g. "11B4S"). For example, engineers received not only one week of conventional demolitions training, but also another one training with expedient unconventional explosives. The weapons specialists received extensive training on numerous foreign weapons. The O&I NCOs were trained in planning Special Forces operations, intelligence techniques, and how to operate agent nets within a guerrilla or counterinsurgency unit. The radiomen learned Morse code, how to operate special radios and use expedient antennas, and long-range communications. The medics were trained much more than any other enlisted medical personnel, to include the treatment of gunshot wounds and amputations.

Phase III lasted six weeks and covered unconventional warfare, organizing guerrilla forces, low-level tradecraft, and other guerrilla-warfare skills. The two-week field-training exercises saw the students organized into 10–12-man "A-teams" (a group of officers and senior NCOs formed to train and lead guerrillas, though in this case the teams were without officers) and conducting an unconventional-warfare exercise in which they trained a small guerrilla force composed of 82nd Airborne Division paratroopers, often from service support units, and then led them on patrols and raids.

Upon graduation they were now "flash-qualified" and sewed on their new Special Forces unit's beret flash. Some went directly to the 5th SFGA in Vietnam, but most were assigned elsewhere: 1st SFGA on Okinawa was responsible for the Pacific and Asia (exclusive of Vietnam and Thailand); 3rd SFGA at Fort Bragg was responsible for Africa; 6th SFGA, also at Fort Bragg, was responsible for the Middle East; 7th SFGA at Fort Bragg was deployable worldwide as a backup unit; 8th SFGA in Panama was responsible for Latin America; 10th SFGA in West Germany was responsible for Europe; and the 46th Special Forces Company was based in Thailand. Training as Special Forces soldiers continued in units, and some men would later be reassigned to the 5th SFGA in Vietnam.

Finding the elusive SOG
MACV–SOG was highly classified, and few Special Forces soldiers knew what it was. There were rumors about SOG's existence and such organizations as CCN, CCC, and CCS and Projects DELTA, OMEGA, and SIGMA (which also conducted covert recon missions), but no one really knew what they were. Special Forces veterans of these activities never spoke of them and told others they overheard talking about them to keep quiet.

Mrs Billye Alexander, popularly known as "Mrs A," worked at the Pentagon's Office of Personnel Operations. She was responsible for assigning Special Forces soldiers to Vietnam. She also identified and assigned selected Special Forces NCOs needed by SOG. Many Special Forces soldiers desiring Vietnam duty simply called Mrs A directly and requested an assignment. So many Special Forces soldiers volunteered for Vietnam that the assignments had to be restricted, even though there were Special Forces shortages in Vietnam, because otherwise other Special Forces units would have been left short of men. There were simply not enough qualified Special Forces soldiers to go around. While few men knew much about SOG or even what it stood for, they heard rumors and sought the assignment.

Once in Vietnam they found that it was just as difficult to learn any more about the mysterious organization. One had to know someone in the unit or be extremely persistent. Those making enquiries were often told to wait until they were assigned to an A-team before pursuing it further. This was a put-off, and anyone understanding how the Army worked knew that once assigned to an A-team it would be even more difficult to be reassigned. The 14-man A-teams manning the many remote strike-force camps were considered "fat" if they had ten men. There was not much of a chance of being let go once a home had been found for them.

Four men of RT Marine of CCN are lifted out by a McGuire-rig extraction system fitted to a 57th Aviation Company UH-1H. The men could not be hoisted into the helicopter, but had to ride below it. (Frank Greco via John Plaster)

After being in-processed through one of the replacement battalions, Special Forces soldiers reported to the 5th SFGA Headquarters at Nha Trang. They were provided with a briefing on Special Forces activities, the strike forces scattered from one end of the country to the other, the Mobile Strike Force Command (MIKE Force)[4], various training operations, and guarded mention might be made of the special reconnaissance projects. There was no mention of SOG, however. Some were more persistent and approached either the sergeant major or an acquaintance who had been in-country for a while, or made inquires at the Project DELTA or GAMMA compounds down the road. They may or may not have had any luck. Some dug deeper and found out where the secreted CCN, CCC, or CCS were located. By determination and subterfuge some made their way to Kontum, Da Nang, or Ban Me Thuot. Technically they were AWOL, but if they could sell themselves they had a home. NCOs who had previously served in Vietnam and had contacts might be asked to sign up for SOG. If replacements were urgently needed then they were asked if they wanted to volunteer for SOG during in-processing.

All Special Forces soldiers assigned to the 5th SFGA were required to undertake the Combat Orientation Course (COC, or "Cock Course") conducted by the MACV Recondo School (an abbreviated Ranger course). This entailed a week of acclimatization and refresher training in land navigation, first aid, communications, directing artillery and air strikes, patrolling, company tactics, working with interpreters, etc. Morning runs with sand-filled rucksacks were the order of the day. The second week saw the class moved to Hon Tre Island. Here they undertook practical exercises in what they had learned the previous week. They also conducted a three-day combat patrol.

Returning to Nha Trang, the Special Forces soldiers received their assignments. Some who had managed to find their way to an SOG base skipped the COC. They would undertake additional training, however. Once accepted by SOG, the new man would be interviewed by the sergeant major and different One-Zeros in order to find a personality and temperament fit. He would be issued uniforms, weapons, and equipment and assigned a fighting position for base defense. Some men might be assigned to staff positions, "Hatchet" platoons, the security company, and so on. It depended on their temperament and where they were needed. Most recon men were weapons or engineering specialists. Fewer were trained in communications or

4 See Battle Orders 30: *Mobile Strike Forces in Vietnam 1966–70.*

The 30ft extraction ladder allowed RTs to be inserted and extracted from LZs and PZs that the helicopter could not land on. The ladders, one on each side (though only one is deployed here), could be dropped through thin trees, brush, and high grass. (Mike Sloniker via John Plaster)

O&I. Even fewer were medics, as these were needed in the strike camps, though a Special Forces medic could conduct a reconnaissance or offensive operation just as effectively as other Special Forces men. Most Special Forces troopers carried a security clearance of "Secret," but those assigned to SOG were eligible for "Top Secret" clearance.

TRAINING

Other than training within their assigned Special Forces groups, there was not a lot of additional training undertaken by Special Forces. Some engineers took courses in the operation of heavy equipment, and some medics undertook additional training, but very few attended Recondo School or Pathfinder School (for tactical air-traffic control). Such skills were already included in Special Forces training. High Altitude Low Opening (HALO)

 ONE-ZERO COURSE, DONG BA THIN

The three-week One-Zero Course covered a wide range of subjects at a fast pace. The sergeant-first-class instructor (**1**), a former One-Zero assigned to Special Forces Detachment B-51, wears the typical duty uniform with the LLDB (Vietnamese special forces) pocket patch and LLDB jump wings over the right pocket. SF troopers assigned to MACV-SOG wore the same uniform, but without the LLDB insignia, which indentified advisers to the LLDB. The student uniform was undershirts in the hot classrooms. Here an orientation is conducted on the KY-38 Nestor secure voice system (**2**) attached to an AN/PRC-77 FM radio (**3**). The KY-38 permitted secure voice communications without the need for encrypting messages using KAC codebooks. The downside was that the AN/PRC-77 and KY-38 together weighed about 50lb. The two units were carried by two different men. The "Key-38" required two BA-386 batteries and the "Prick-77" required one, which meant a large number of the heavy spare batteries had to be carried (**4**). The KY-38 had to be reset every day using the KYK-38 mechanical key-fill device (not shown), which reset the pins in the 64 holes seen in the open mechanical-memory-system cover (**5**).

parachute-jump training and scuba training were limited at the time. A number of men did attend Ranger School, and Ranger-qualified Special Forces NCOs were found throughout SOG.

One-Zero Course

Regardless of what an SOG recon man may have learned in infantry AIT, from serving in an infantry unit, the Ranger Course, the COC, or any other training, he still had a lot to learn. All of his past training and experience was of course applicable and valuable, but there were several unique aspects to SOG operations. First, they were conducted "across the fence," in Laos and Cambodia, where the US officially had no troops. They operated without artillery or close air support, something few US units ever risked doing, though they did receive this support when operating in South Vietnam. They seldom had direct radio contact with bases, relying on communications relay aircraft flying on the Vietnamese side of the border. These were C-130 airborne battlefield command-and-control centers, designated "Hillsboro" during the day and "Moonbeam" at night. This caused further delays in requesting desperately needed extraction aircraft and attack helicopters. While any reconnaissance patrol could find itself deep among enemy forces, SOG RTs routinely went into heavy occupied and controlled base areas with the enemy expecting their presence. Specialized counter-reconnaissance units were fielded to hunt down RTs and large numbers of combat and service troops would be turned out. The RTs seldom numbered over nine men and had to be able to fight viciously and give the impression of being a larger force than they really were.

All Americans assigned to RTs underwent One-Zero training, which qualified them both for RT duty and as an RT leader, after the requisite mission experience. There were many instances of new men being assigned to RTs and sent on missions prior to attending One-Zero training. They were of course fully briefed, and they rehearsed with the RT during its pre-mission preparations. They would still be sent on the course as soon as possible even though they might have a number of missions under their belts.

The course was conducted at Dong Ba Thin, located between Nha Trang and Cam Ranh Bay under Special Forces Detachment B-51. It was here that Vietnamese Special Forces (LLDB) were trained, along with the MIKE Force jump school. The three-week course ran seven days a week. There was no room for slow learners and they were expected to be sharp and flexible. The instructors were all former One-Zeros. Classes contained 20 or more men and might include a few Special Forces members from other reconnaissance forces.

One-Zero instruction included: survival, escape and evasion, resistance to interrogation, advanced first aid, immediate-action drills (IADs), silenced weapons, detecting booby traps, setting booby traps, demolitions, defensive and offensive use of Claymores, arm and hand signals, determining friendly and enemy personnel, target identification, radio procedures, use of spotter aircraft, directing air strikes, AN/URC-10 emergency radio, patrol procedures, working with indigenous troops, using an interpreter, mission planning, mission briefback[5], post-mission debriefing, and more.

---

5 A mission briefback was conducted just before a mission launched. The team would brief the commander or operations officer on how they were going to conduct the mission from insertion to extraction, and demonstrate that they had covered all contingencies and were adequately prepared and equipped to accomplish the mission.

A two-day mission was conducted prior to graduation in order to practice skills and procedures. Team leaders were rotated in each of the RTs and a quick field debriefing was undertaken after each rotation, with every man having a turn as the One-Zero. A simple graduation ceremony was held in the mess hall, where each man received a certificate, quickly returned to his FOB, and went to work.

It was common for a snap link to be attached to the right shoulder of the suspenders, and a fighting or utility knife attached to the left shoulder strap. Note the colored- and white-smoke grenades on the right side of the belt along with M26 fragmentation grenades. (Jay Massey via Steve Sherman)

RT training

The One-Zero was responsible for training his RT. There was no collective training of all RTs. Training was routine and generally conducted at a relaxed pace, depending on mission tempo. With two or three mission runs each month the RTs kept sharp. Training picked up when a new man, American or indigenous, was assigned. Replacements had to be be fully integrated into the team and understand all of its tactics, techniques, and procedures.

RT movement formations were simple. Because they normally traveled in dense foliage they used a column. The distance between men varied depending on visibility, but they were fairly close in order to preclude accidental separation. In light vegetation they would move in a staggered formation with alternating men a meter or so right and left of the centerline. Crossing dangerous areas such as roads, trails, or streams required caution. Some RTs crossed one man at a time in single file after first possibly sending a man to check the far side. This was dangerous if the enemy opened fire with the RT split on opposite sides of the obstacle. Most found the best way was to get on line and all cross at once. This also reduced the chance of individuals being separated. Once across the danger area the RT might pause long enough to listen for enemy activity and then move out quickly to get away from the area. Crossing obstacles that slowed movement (e.g. a steep-sided stream, extremely dense and tangled underbrush, or a deep gully) demanded precautions. The first men across could not simply keep going; they had to wait for the others to make their way across.

Recon men typically undertook practice firing every other day. This consisted of close-range rapid-fire, accuracy firing, rapid-reloading practice, or live-fire IADs. The One-Zero took his team out to a secluded area and they moved through terrain with different densities of vegetation to practice movement formations and IADs. The One-Zero would shout "Contact" and a direction (front, right, left, or rear) and the RT would respond to the supposed threat. Some RTs carried a magazine of tracers or one with every other round being a tracer. They opened fire in rapid three- or five-round bursts, and the swarm of tracers, coupled with bursting grenades, would rattle the enemy, experienced or not.

How the RT reacted to the threat depended on the terrain and amount of fire they were under. SOPs varied, but the following was typical. The immediate response was for everyone who could bear their weapons in the direction of enemy to open fire with everything they had. If the

B   RT TRAINING WITH INDIGENOUS PERSONNEL IN VIETNAM

RT training was continuous, in order to perfect and improve the team's skills and implement lessons learned from earlier missions. This six-man RT practices the "banana peel" IAD. It was designed as a means to break contact rapidly and maintain continuous fire on what was hopefully a surprised and at least momentarily disorganized enemy. The maneuver calls for the point man, or whoever detected the enemy first, to open fire immediately on full-automatic while the second man in line throws a WP grenade in order to blind the enemy. In training a burning-type AN-M8 white-smoke grenade was thrown instead. The grenadier begins pumping out high-explosive rounds as fast as possible. The point man (here wearing an NVA uniform and gear to confuse the enemy further) darts back to the rear, running down the column's center – each man has stepped to the right or left to make a lane. Each man continued to fire and throw fragmentation grenades before he too peeled back. This process was repeated until contact was broken with the dispirited enemy, and the team would then change direction frequently as they moved to their PZ. Such IADs were rehearsed over and over with simulated attacks from any direction until it became second nature. Such exercises were conducted every 1–3 weeks, along with the test firing of weaponry, thus allowing ammunition to be replaced.

RT Michigan of CCN rushes across a bomb-blasted area and into cover. This shows how canteens and colored-smoke grenades were carried on the back of rucksacks. Note the coiled utility rope on the second man's belt. (Ken Bowra via John Plaster)

enemy fire was heavy, SOPs often specified that every man fired at least five magazines while grenadiers fired as rapidly as possible, launching a grenade every 2–3 seconds. The idea was to gain fire superiority and make the enemy believe they were facing a larger force in order to confuse them and make them keep their heads down as the RT broke contact. For an engagement from the flank the RT turned in that direction and open fired while on-line. If engaged from the front or rear the RT conducted a "peel-back" or "banana peel." The point man emptied a magazine and threw a grenade and ran to the rear, reloading, as the second man then emptied a magazine and threw a grenade. One of these may have been white phosphorus (WP) to blind and panic the enemy. Odd-numbered men stepped to the right and even-numbered men to the left to leave a "lane" down the center of the formation. Some men might throw grenades to the sides, discouraging anyone attempting to flank them. Each man would peel back after firing and take up a position to the rear on-line to mass their fire or repeat another peel-back. This would continue until the One-Zero ordered them to run for it once they had enough breathing room. This was his judgment call. Care had to be taken to prevent separation and hitting one another. A Claymore or grenade with a one-minute delay fuse might be set on the back-trail as well as trip-wired grenades. The point man and rearguard usually carried a pre-rigged Claymore for this purpose.

The RT would then change direction and head for the nearest pick-up zone (PZ). Each American team member was aware of where these were in relation to the day's planned route. Of course, the enemy also knew where suitable clearings were and would possibly head in that direction or send units to occupy them. If a PZ was found to be occupied then the team would have to try another one, head east to South Vietnam (which the enemy expected), or turn back into enemy territory in the hope of losing their pursuers, where they would hide out and wait for things to cool down. While on the move they would attempt to make contact with a radio-relay aircraft and request extraction.

Occupying a "remain overnight" position (RON) was also practiced during RT training. Some One-Zeros selected the RON site, passed it, then fish-hooked back to occupy it and ambush any enemy in pursuit. Others made a direction change off their course and occupied the RON by halting where the One-Zero ordered. RONs would be occupied at dusk, when reduced visibility made it difficult to see what the RT was doing, but when there was still enough light for them to emplace Claymores and study the ground in front of them. RONs well away from streams were selected as the noise of the water could mask the enemy's approach.

RTs also conducted training on radio procedures, first aid, land navigation, air–ground signaling, and any other skills the One-Zero felt needed improving. Changes or enhancements to their SOP based on lessons learned were practiced, as were rehearsals for special mission requirements such as a prisoner snatches or wiretapping.

A 158th Assault Helicopter Battalion UH-1H brings out a CCN RT from Laos with two of the team hooked onto the aluminum extraction ladder with snap hooks on their harnesses. (Mike Sloniker via John Plaster)

The unofficial patches of CCN, CCC, and CCS. These gaudy insignia were not worn on uniforms, but often on "party jackets" worn when off duty, and painted on unit signs. (Author's collection)

APPEARANCE

Rather than muscle-bound Rambos, Special Forces troopers tended to be lean and of average height, but as in any group, they came in all shapes and sizes. Recon men were typically in their 20s, but some were in their early 30s. However, with the extreme physical and physiological demands inherent in their missions, it was a young man's enterprise. Many kept their hair cut short because of the heat and for cleanliness, but some grew their hair longish. Mustaches were uncommon, mainly because Special Forces sergeants major tended to frown on them. Tattoos were uncommon and discouraged in Special Forces in order not to advertise who they were. There were few African-Americans and only small numbers of Hispanics in SOG.

The standard uniform worn at an FOB was olive-green jungle fatigues and jungle boots with a green beret. The beret was adorned by the 5th SFGA flash, even though SOG was not part of the 5th. The USSF patch and airborne tab was worn on the left shoulder, jump wings and Combat Infantryman Badge over the left chest pocket and the "US ARMY" tape, while the nametape was over the right chest pocket. SOG personnel were not awarded the honorary LLDB jump wings, as were 5th SFGA personnel, as they were not advisers to the LLDB. Nor did members of SOG wear the LLDB patch on the left chest pocket. Rank chevrons were worn centered on the upper sleeves. From 1968 subdued pin-on or sew-on rank insignia could be worn on the collars, but Special Forces soldiers tended to retain the sleeve insignia. Additionally, while subdued insignia were authorized, Special Forces retained full-color insignia on jungle fatigues, viewing them as a "garrison" uniform. They were to appear as other Special Forces personnel and wore no insignia identifying them as belonging to SOG. Prior to deployment to Vietnam each soldier was issued three sets of tropical combat uniforms. These consisted of jungle fatigues, five sets of olive-drab undershirts and undershorts, two olive-drab towels, and two pairs of tropical combat boots.

There was no "standard" mission uniform. Uniforms were "sterile," meaning that their national origin could not be identified. No insignia of any form was worn. The most common were US jungle fatigues with labels removed, which could be mistaken for the NVA's dark-green uniforms. Usually the "jungles" were camouflaged by lightly spray-painting irregular black bands

C **RON**

At sunset the RT would seek a suitable site in which to "remain overnight." RONs were selected some distance from trails, streams, gullies, or natural movement routes. Sometimes the smallest possible clump of brush was selected, in the hope that searchers might think that the brush patch was too small to hide an RT. Hidden in dense brush – stripped away here to depict the RT's position – they would form a "wagon wheel," sitting back-to-back leaning against their rucksacks or lying prone facing head-out and close enough to alert each other with the tap of a boot. One man at a time would stealthily creep out and emplace his Claymore mine 10–30yds away on the other side of a substantial tree to protect the RT from its blast and secondary fragmentation. He would retain the firing device in his pocket and connect it upon returning to the team. If the enemy approached a RON then they would blow all their Claymores simultaneously and break out in a clock direction ordered by the One-Zero. They might hold their fire in order to prevent the enemy from knowing which direction they were headed. The direction the One-Zero faced was designated "12 o'clock," and that was the planned direction in which they would move out in the morning. Breaking out of a RON and evading the enemy in the dark could easily result in team members becoming separated, and efforts were made to keep everyone together, especially since the RT would typically make misleading changes of direction away from the RON.

Tiger-stripe camouflage was seldom worn by RTs, but in some cases it was. "Tigers" offered effective concealment in much of Vietnam's vegetation, especially bamboo. These men wear triangular bandages as sweatbands. Both men are armed with XM177E2 submachine guns mounting XM148 grenade launchers. (James Bolen via Steve Sherman)

on them. This was often done with one man spraying the other after they had donned their uniforms and web gear. Laundering removed much of the paint, and uniforms were resprayed before each mission. The lower legs were saturated with insect repellent in order to deter leeches. Some individuals sewed additional pockets on their shirtsleeves. Trousers were altered to make them tight fitting, which prevented them from getting snagged on vegetation and making noise.

Some RTs wore NVA-style uniforms. From a distance an American could be mistaken for Vietnamese in such a uniform and among shadows and vegetation. Black, khaki (actually light brown), and dark-green uniforms were procured for this purpose. In some instances green jungle fatigues were dyed black. Some teams would outfit the point man in an NVA uniform, including an AK-47 and chest magazine pouches, in order to give an unexpectedly encountered enemy a moment's pause. The rearguard too might be so uniformed. The black uniforms were effective at night, but stood out in daylight among the green vegetation.

Tiger-stripe camouflage, worn by the Civilian Irregular Defense Group (CIDG)[6], was not generally used by SOG as it was too readily identified as a pattern used by Free World forces. However, "tigers" were sometimes worn by some RTs operating in thick underbrush, where they were very effective. They were sometimes worn when conducting training outside the base camp so it would be assumed that they belonged to the CIDG.

Undershirts and underwear were seldom worn as they trapped sweat and causing chafing and rashes. Some men even wore no socks. Dog tags, ID cards, and other items that might indicate the recon man's name or nationality were prohibited.

Some RTs insisted that all members wear the same type of headgear, as this improved friend-or-foe recognition when silhouetted at night. Others allowed individual preference. Most wore the full-brim "boonie hat," which was relatively shapeless, comfortable, and provided protection from sun and rain. Most were olive green or had a camouflage pattern. Some men had orange marker-panel material sewn into the inside of the hat. They could turn the inside of the hat toward an aircraft and "flash" it by opening and closing the hat. They could also turn the hat inside out to aid being spotted by an extraction aircraft. Some men wore headscarves made from olive-drab triangular bandages, a simple cloth triangle. These were also used as neck scarves or "drive-on rags," as were wide strips of olive-drab towels. With NVA uniforms they usually wore black or green boonie hats or, in rare istances, tan or light-green NVA pith helmets. In some areas the NVA instituted a "color of the day" policy, with hats specifying which color would be worn on which days at irregular intervals. An RT in the area of operations (AO) would be on the lookout each morning to see what color was being worn that day. Trouser belts might be an issue black web belt, a 15ft olive-drab web A7A cargo strap cut to belt length, a triangular bandage folded into a belt, or a doubled length of nylon climbing rope knotted, which could also be used for other purposes.

6 The CIDG was a body of locally raised troops advised by Special Forces personnel.

Standard jungle boots were usually worn, but sometimes Canadian-made Bata boots were used as they had similar soles to some NVA boots. Jungle boots had a distinctive sole pattern and efforts were made to develop boots with less distinctive soles. This included soles that looked like an indigenous bare foot, a truck-tire pattern known as "Ho Chi Minh sandals," and even a leaf-impression pattern. Such efforts failed as they provided poor traction, were uncomfortable, and they lost their effect when worn down. On occasion thick socks were pulled over boots or they were wrapped in burlap. These wore out quickly, provided bad traction, and made for difficult walking when wet. Efforts to obscure tracks with leafy branches greatly disturbed ground cover and attracted the attention of even inexperienced trackers to the path. In areas where land leeches were particularly bad, some men wore World War II leggings over their boots with their trousers bloused into them.

Camouflage sticks, or "cami sticks," were carried by each man, the most common being colored loam and light green, with a color on each end. Loam was used on the high facial areas that would reflect light: the forehead, cheekbones, nose, jaw line, chin, and ears. Light green was used around the eyes, lower cheeks, and neck. The back of the neck, hands, and wrists were also camouflaged. Most military equipment was dark-colored, usually in olive drab, but some items were not subdued or were glossy. These would be spray-painted or worked over with a camouflage stick.

Part of the art of camouflage was ensuring that gear was silent, with no metal-on-metal noise, creaking, or jingling. Equipment was padded against soft items placed between harder ones. Other items were protected by tape or rubber bands. One item, named "100mph tape" because it was required to remain attached to a surface in a 100mph wind, was a form of early duct tape that was preferred, as it was colored green or dark olive drab. Black plastic electrical tape was sometimes used to secure items, but this had the disadvantage of being glossy.

Smell was also an issue. Scented soap and aftershave was not used before missions. There was no washing, shaving, or teeth-brushing during a mission. Food was not heated and no coffee or cocoa was prepared. Food and heating-tablet smells were avoided. Insect repellent had an odor too, but this was faint.

US recon team One-Zeros and One-Ones. Note the green 2in.-wide "100mph tape" affixed to the M16A1 rifle. Three men wear strobe-light cases on their right shoulders. The man to the far right wears a black VC uniform. (James Bolen via Steve Sherman)

EQUIPMENT AND WEAPONS

Individual equipment

The equipment, or "web gear," carried by recon men varied greatly and changed over time. There was no standard SOG assemblage. Some RTs were allowed individual preference in addition to what their job, weapon, and mission required. Other RTs had specific standards regarding what and where items were carried in order to allow critical gear to be recovered from casualties.

Recon men carried their equipment in layers. The first layer was carried on their person, in their pockets. If they lost their web gear and rucksack they still retained essential items on their person. This included a pocket knife, two compasses, a watch, a map, a notepad and pen, morphine syrettes, an emergency radio, and various air–ground signal devices. The compasses, carried in a pocket, might have been attached to the uniform by a "dummy cord."

The next layer was the web gear or load-bearing equipment (LBE). There was a great deal of variance here, but they were based on two systems. A favorite was the World War II Browning Automatic Rifle (BAR) belt. Four XM177/M16 magazines could fit into each of its six pockets. Typically five pockets held magazines and one held items the bearer wished to retain if he lost his rucksack. Air–ground marker items might have been carried in that pocket. Canteen carriers, first-aid pouches, and other pouches were attached

 ONE-ZERO'S ON-PERSON LOAD

The equipment carried by One-Zero John Plaster (CCC), the SOG chronicler, included a great deal of gear. Other American RT members carried essentially the same equipment, although grenades and other munitions might differ. This plate displays the equipment carried on his person, mainly in uniform pockets. The equipment carried in his rucksack and in his web gear is depicted in Plates E and F, respectively. Plaster carries a 5.56mm XM177E2 submachine gun loaded with the only 30-round magazine he possesses. He wears sterile US jungle fatigues, which have been camouflaged with black spray-paint. Extra pockets have been sewn onto his sleeves.

1. Map covered by acetate

2. AN/URC-10 emergency radio

3. Wristwatch

4. Wrist compass

5. Lensatic compass

6. Pilot-type pen flashlight

7. SDU-5/E strobe light

8. M186 pen flare projector with seven flares

9. Mini colored-smoke grenade

10. Mk III air–ground signal mirror

11. Air–ground signal panel (cut from larger VS-17 marker panel)

12. Pocket knife

13. Whistle

14. Camouflage stick

15. Anti-malaria tablets in plastic bottle

16. Salt tablets in plastic bottle

17. Four morphine syrettes in plastic bottle

18. Notepad and pen in plastic bag

18

7

17

2

15

16

14

13

8

4

12

11

1

3

6

10

5

9

A recon team poses beside its insertion Huey, along with the flight crew. This is a rare instance in which most RT members were armed with silenced M3 "grease guns." Note that a snap link is attached to the rucksack shoulder straps to allow them to be hooked to extraction ropes or ladders, which was safer than keeping them on one's back when being extracted. The silver tubes strapped atop some rucksacks are handheld "pop-up" signal flares. (James Bolen via Steve Sherman)

to the BAR belt. Some men cut off the two back pockets and sewed on canteen carriers. Most men carried two 1qt plastic canteens with small bottles of halazone water-purification tablets taped to the cap's retaining strap. Since food or beverages were not heated some soldiers did not carry a canteen cup.

The other LBE systems were the M1956 cotton gear and the similar M1967 nylon gear, which were developed for Vietnam. These items were often mixed in web-gear sets. The pouches and carriers were attached to a pistol belt. M1956 ammunition pouches held four 20-round XM177 magazines, four 30-round carbine magazines, or three 40mm grenades. It was too deep for M16 magazines, so a field dressing was often placed in the bottom to raise the magazines. The M1967 nylon pouch was similar, as well as a shallow version to accommodate XM177 magazines. A grenade could be attached to either end of these pouches. Many recon men did not use ammunition pouches, but rather canteen carriers with up to six on a belt. Five XM177 or six M2 carbine magazines could be held in a canteen carrier, as could four hand grenades or six 40mm grenades. A first-aid or survival kit was often attached to the back center of the belt.

This ammunition was heavy; 20 fully loaded M16 magazines weighed 14lb. Suspenders were attached to take the weight off the hips, onto which first-aid kits, compass pouches, grenades, and other items could be attached.

The number of magazines carried varied according to an RT's SOP, mission requirements, and individual preference. A typical magazine load for a man armed with an XM177 was one 30-round magazine and 20 20-round magazines, totaling 450 rounds. This number is based on full magazines, but most men carried one or two fewer rounds in their magazine to prevent straining the follower spring. Some men placed a tracer as the third round from the bottom to signal that the magazine was nearly empty. Strips of 100mph tape were fastened to the bottom of magazines as pull-tabs. They were placed into pouches mouth down to help keep out dirt, and with the bullets pointed away from the body in the event that pouches were hit and rounds detonated.

A soldier typically carried four to six fragmentation grenades and two WP grenades, along with two to four colored-smoke grenades. One or two smoke grenades were carried on the web gear and the rest on the outside of the rucksack. A few V40 mini fragmentation grenades might be carried as well. Grenades were carried on the ends of magazine pouches, in canteen carriers, Claymore bags, pockets (V40s), or attached to their belt suspenders. Some men straightened the arming pins and warped them with electrical tape. This allowed them to use the grenade while holding their weapon or with a wounded arm. They yanked off the tape with their teeth and then pulled the pin with their teeth. The safety clip would be thumbed open. An eight-man RT might carry 80 fragmentation and WP grenades and about 30 40mm grenades per grenadier. That translates into a great deal of firepower in a firefight. Most grenadiers wore the grenade-carrier vest with 18 high-explosive grenade and four pyrotechnic pockets.

Knives were carried more as utility tools than as weapons. Common makes included Randall Models 14 and 16, Baker SOG Recon, Gerber Mk II, Marine Ka-Bar, and Air Force survival knives. Pocket knives were carried too.

Vietnamese rucksacks were provided by the Counterinsurgency Support Office (CISO). These were modeled after an NVA rucksack, so they were ideal for deception purposes. They were made of gray-green or olive-drab colored waterproofed canvas and had three external pockets. They were of a crude and simple design, with the shoulder straps' ends simply knotted to buckles. It had a flap-covered, strap-secured main compartment. They had no support frame, making it uncomfortable with a heavy load. Their relatively small size limited their load and thus mission duration. The CISO also procured hammocks, ponchos, poncho liners, lightweight sleeping bags, and other gear sized for Asians and produced at low cost. These were not as durable as US gear and the green and gray-green colors varied widely. In northern Vietnam and Laos the night could be cold, making poncho liners, sleeping bags, and sleeping sweaters necessary. The lightweight sleeping bag consisted of a flannel-lined, water-resistant rectangular cover closed by snaps on one side and at the foot end.

Other gear was distributed through the team and might have included an Olympus Pen EE 35mm camera, a 20x M49 observation telescope, one or two pairs of 6x30 M13A1 or 7x50 M15A1, M16, or M17A1 binoculars, occasionally an AN/PVS-1 or -2 starlight scope, and, when conducting a wiretap mission, a voice-activated General Electric 8-track cassette tape recorder with wiretapping leads. Some individuals carried additional medical supplies, such as field dressings, gauze pads and rolls, adhesive tape, morphine syrettes, IV saline solution, serum-albumin cans, and codeine cough syrup. Most carried a "One-Zero med kit" or what was simply called a "pill bottle." This was a large plastic pill bottle containing anti-malaria, salt, aspirin, Darvon 65, Lomotil, penicillin, and dextro-emphetamine tablets all mixed together. These were shared with the indigenous troops. Additional demolition materials and even M21 antitank mines might have been required for some missions. Items necessary for prisoner snatches included tie-locks, handcuffs, sandbags (used as hoods), and blindfolds.

The XM28 mask protected only from tear gas, but it was compact and light as opposed to the bulky and heavy M17 gas mask. RTs carried them for protection from their own tear-gas grenades and because areas along the Ho Chi Minh Trail were dusted with aerial-delivered tear-gas powder that could be stirred up when passing through foliage.

Usually only one radio was taken, carried by the One-One, but sometimes a second was carried by the One-Two. In some instances the One-Zero preferred to carry a radio, especially if two were carried. Radios were the RT's lifeline to report their location or intelligence, and call for air support or extraction. The 26lb AN/PRC-10 radio was used initially. It was complex to operate, requiring manual calibration, and it rapidly burned through batteries. Its range was only 3–5 miles. In 1966 the AN/PRC-25 was introduced. It was simple to operate, more reliable, and less battery-hungry. It weighed 24lb and had a range of at least 5 miles. The AN/PRC-77 of 1968 differed in having an attachment for a KY-38 secure-voice device, and this began to be used by SOG. The "25" was transistorized while the "10" used vacuum tubes.

 ONE-ZERO RUCKSACK GEAR

The typical contents of a One-Zero's indigenous rucksack, based on the NVA rucksack, contained mission and personal-sustainment items. The demolition materials (1–4) were for targets of opportunity and could also be used to break contact with the enemy. The Claymore mine was for securing a RON and breaking contact. The delay fuses could be used on the Claymore when breaking contact. The poncho shown here (15) is a gray-green indigenous model, but a heavier and larger olive-drab US model might have been used. The lightweight sleeping bag (16), which was flannel-lined and had a water-resistant cover, might be substituted by a gray-green indigenous poncho liner or a slightly larger woodland-pattern camouflaged US poncho liner. A gray-green sleeping shirt (17), a pullover sweater-like garment, was sometimes carried. Northern Cambodia and southeast Laos could experience chilly and sometimes wet nights. Olive-drab 37 x 37 x 52in. triangular bandages were worn as headbands, neck scarves, belts, as weapon slings, and even as a means to secure prisoners.

1. Two M112 1¼lb C4 demolition charges
2. Two M60 fuse igniters and two 14in. (40-second) time-delay fuses
3. Four M7 non-electric blasting caps in protective 10-cap box
4. M2 blasting-cap crimper
5. M18A1 Claymore mine, M57 firing device, and 100ft M4 firing-wire spool
6. M34 WP grenade
7. M18 violet- and yellow-smoke grenades
8. Customized jungle first-aid kit
9. 2qt collapsible canteen
10. Two 1qt canteens
11. Ten PIR or LRP meals (one of each pictured)
12. Small machete
13. Two tie-lock hand restraints
14. Insect repellent
15. Lightweight poncho
16. Lightweight sleeping bag
17. Sleeping shirt
18. Indigenous rucksack

18

11

4

13

8

6

15

16

17

3

9

1

14

4

2

10

5

7

12

M18
SMOK
LOW

M18
SMOK
VADLET

FRONT
TOWARD ENEMY

Voice-activated General Electric cassette-tape recorders were used to record NVA field-telephone conversations during wiretap missions. This first-generation wiretap used alligator clips connected to the telephone wire and required the insulation to be stripped. The second-generation tap used thin wires that were slid into the insulation. The third-generation tap used an induction clamp folded over the wire, without tampering with the insulation at all. Wiretaps helped determine convoy schedules on the Trail. (John Plaster)

Both radios were FM and called the "Prick-10" or "Prick-25." They normally used a 3ft-long flexible tape antenna. A collapsible long antenna increased the range by a few miles, but it was impossible to walk with through foliage with the 10ft-long whip antenna. A spare battery was carried for each planned day of the mission's duration. Radios were monitored during the day but turned off at night in the RON. The radio operator carried the signal operating instructions (SOI) with call signs, daily and alternate frequencies, and the KAC codebook.

American team members carried pocket-sized emergency radios. These were small and lightweight, and transmitted voice or a continuous-wave homing beacon on a single preset guard frequency: 243.0 MHz. Their range was 10 miles in voice mode and longer in beacon mode. An extraction aircraft could home in on the beacon tone and then two-way voice contact was established to pinpoint the RT's location. These radios were used only if the main radio was lost or damaged.

Weapons

Light and compact weapons were necessary for the heavily loaded RTs, but an even more critical factor was firepower. If they were detected then an RT had to make its way to a PZ as rapidly as possible and call for immediate extraction. This took time, at least an hour, and if engaged they required significant firepower to have even a slight chance of surviving. The ability of weapons to penetrate through brush and bamboo was an important consideration for RTs, as they operated among dense vegetation in an effort to remain undetected.

An initial requirement was that the weapons carried on missions into Laos and Cambodia could not be of American manufacture. This was to ensure plausible deniability of US involvement. This restriction was lifted in 1967, by which time US weapons were wider spread. There were exceptions, such as the M2 carbine and .45-cal. pistol, as these weapons had long been in use in the region. Weapons usually had their serial numbers ground off.

The first standard weapon was the Swedish Carl Gustav m/45b submachine gun (aka the "Swedish-K" or "K-gun"[7]) procured by the CIA. It was compact, with a folding stock, making it only 21.7in. long when collapsed and 31.1in. long when extended. It weighed 7.3lb, but 9.2lb loaded with a 36-round magazine. It was rugged and reliable. However, the 9mm round had poor penetration through brush and bamboo. Sweden, in protest against the war, placed an arms embargo on the US in 1966 and the K-gun supply dried up.

The Korean War-era .30-cal. M2 carbine was also used initially. It was light and compact, weighing 5.7lb and being only 3ft long. It was a selective-fire weapon and had a 30-round magazine. Its problem was that it fired

7 The "K" is derived from *Kulsprutepistol* (machine pistol).

Indigenous members of a CCS RT pose before a 2½-ton M135 cargo truck. Most are armed with XM177E2 submachine guns and have taped the muzzles. Two carry M79 grenade launchers and one an M16A1 rifle to provide a longer-ranged weapon. (A. J. Sharp)

the .30-cal. cartridge, which was underpowered, offered only a short range, and obtained poor penetration through dense brush and bamboo. It was not very accurate and overheated rapidly when fired on full automatic. A shortened version was sometimes field-modified. The barrel was cut down almost to the end of the forearm and the shoulder stock was cut off, leaving the pistol grip. There was no front sight. This weapon was notoriously inaccurate and created a great deal of muzzle blast and recoil. It was strictly a "pray and spray" weapon of marginal effectiveness, being useful only for suppressive fire under ranges of 20yds. It was usually carried by a cord around the neck with the weapon hanging at waist level.

A very heavily armed RT New York of CCN, with three Americans and nine indigenous members. Most carry XM177E2 submachine guns, but other weapons include two 40mm M79 grenade launchers (front right, back left), a .30-cal. M2 carbine with M8 grenade launcher fitted with an M34 WP grenade on a launcher adapter (back row, second from left), an RPG-2 grenade launcher (front left), a cut-down 60mm mortar (front row, third from right), and an American with a 7.62mm RPD light machine gun (front row, second from right). (Martin Bennett via John Plaster)

Some RTs carried AK-47 and AKM assault rifles. These were mainly Chinese-made Type 56 copies. AKs weighed 7.5lb and were 35in. in length. There were distinct advantages to using AKs; they reinforced the impression that an RT seen from a distance was NVA/VC, and ammunition and magazines taken from enemy dead could be used. In a chance encounter with the enemy, the sound of AK shots would not necessarily cause a reaction among other enemy in the area. Additionally, the AK was a very effective and reliable weapon, with good penetration through foliage.

Another Soviet-designed weapon used by some RTs was the RPD light machine gun. This 14.5lb bipod-mounted weapon was one of the lightest machine guns in use. It fired the same ammunition as the AK and used a 100-round belt in a drum magazine. Some had the barrel cut back to the gas tube and the bipod removed, reducing its 40.8in. length by about 8in. and knocking off a few pounds of weight. The shortened RPD provided an RT with considerable firepower while weighing about 11lb less than an M60 machine gun.

CIA-procured silenced submachine guns were mainly used for prisoner snatches. One of the most popular was the British 9mm Sten Mk IIS, as it was light at 7.5lb and could be broken down to be carried in a rucksack and assembled before the snatch. Other suppressed weapons were the .45-cal. M3 "grease gun," 9mm Carl Gustav m/45S, Israeli 9mm Uzi, and the M16A1 with a Sionics suppressor. With the exception of the Uzi, these silencers were permanently fitted and impossible to remove in the field, lengthening the

ONE-ZERO'S WEB-GEAR LOAD

The top web gear set (**1**) is based on an M1937 BAR belt and nylon M1967 suspenders, with a WP grenade taped to its left shoulder strap and a snap link on the right shoulder strap; the left pouches and the first on the right held four XM177 magazines each (with a field dressing in each to raise the magazines) plus a notepad in the front pouch on the right, an AN/URC-10 radio in second pouch from the right, and the third from the right was cut off and an M1967 canteen carrier attached. An M1942 first-aid pouch held three mini-fragmentation grenades. A Browning Hi-Power pistol was carried in an M1 holster for the .45-cal. M1911A1 pistol. On the right, below the pouches, is an M1910 canteen carrier with six XM177 magazines. Some recon men carried an empty canteen carrier in which to quickly shove empty magazines rather than trying to place them in magazine-filled pouches. The middle web-gear set (**2**) consists of an M1956 web belt with two M14 magazine pouches, two carriers with 1qt canteens, three M1956 canteen carriers (two for magazines and one for grenades), along with M1956 suspenders on which are placed an XM28 protective-mask case and M34 WP and M7A2 tear-gas grenades. The bottom web gear set (**3**) is composed of an M1956 belt, old-style M16 magazine pouches, M1956 canteen carriers, a strobe light, a first-aid pouch, a serum-albumin can, and a snap link on the M1956 suspenders.

4. FN-Browning Hi-Power pistol with 13-round magazine

5. 20 20-round XM177E2 magazines (380 rounds in total)

6. Two 1qt canteens with halazone tablets

7. XM28 tear-gas protective mask and case

8. Six M67 fragmentation grenades

9. Three V40 mini-fragmentation grenades

10. M34 WP grenade

11. M7A2 tear-gas grenade

12. Leather gloves with the fingers cut off

13. Two snap links

14. Two field dressings

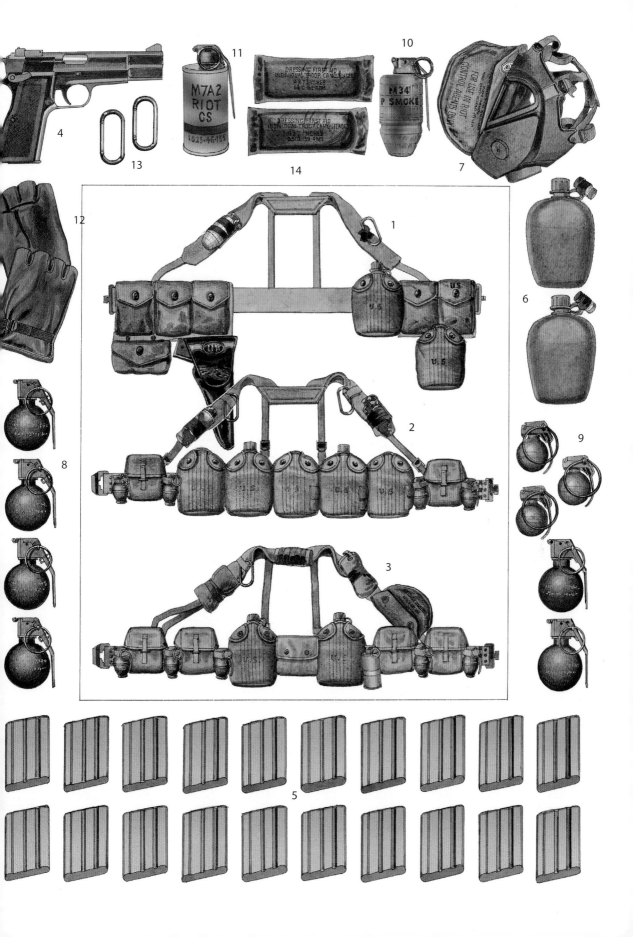

weapon considerably and increasing its weight. These weapons were not effectively suppressed if fired on full automatic, as the working of the bolt and firing mechanism made too much noise, and the buffers within the silencers wore out rapidly. They were normally fired on semi-automatic mode using as few rounds as necessary.

The Belgium-made FN-Browning 9mm Hi-Power pistol was standard, and was CIA-procured. It was very reliable and had a 13-round magazine. Many men carried it attached to a cord around their neck and hanging on their chest inside their shirt. Others carried their pistol in a trousers cargo pocket or canteen carrier. It was always attached by a dummy cord. Some individuals carried Colt .45-cal. M1911A1 pistols with a 7-round magazine. Privately acquired .45-cal. and 9mm pistols were also used, as were revolvers.

From 1968 the primary RT weapons were the 5.56mm XM177E1 and XM177E2 submachine guns. These were shortened-barrel, telescoping-stock versions of the M16A1 rifle. Both weapons used 20-round magazines; few 30-round magazines were available. While the XM177 was lighter and more compact, its penetration through vegetation was poor and it was less accurate and shorter ranged than the M16. For better control on full-auto, some men attached a pistol grip to the forearm. Some RTs carried one or two M16A1s to obtain longer range. The XM177 (the "Colt Commando" or CAR-15) was well liked. If kept clean it was reliable enough. While some RTs were entirely armed with XM177s, there were not always enough available so a mix of weapons was carried. Early on only the Americans had them, with the indigenous men carrying Swedish-Ks or M16s.

Grenade launchers gave an RT an edge in combat as they were effective in keeping the enemy down and disorganizing him. A rapid number of high-explosive rounds confused the enemy and made him believe he had engaged a larger force. The 40mm M79 shoulder-fired, single-shot grenade launcher weighed only 5.95lb and allowed high-explosive rounds to be fired 150yds away at point targets and at a range of up to 375yds for area fire. There was also a canister (buckshot) round with a 35yds range, though it was not very effective in brush nor did it have much shot spread. Various colored-smoke and flare rounds were available. The M79 was sometimes modified by cutting the barrel down by 3in., removing the rear sight, and sawing off the butt stock, leaving a pistol grip. It was inaccurate and lacked range, but it was used for breaking contact at short range. The cut-down M79 was carried on a neck cord or in a canvas holster. A grenadier may or may not have carried a submachine gun, but he would at least have carried a pistol. Two under-barrel grenade launchers were tested, the XM148 of 1967 and XM203 of 1968, mounted under the M16A1 or XM177E2 barrel.

Weapon slings were removed and replaced by cords or triangular bandages tied to the sling swivels. Conventional wisdom called for slings to be removed, as the weapon should always be held at the ready and never slung. The reality was that there were times that a recon man needed both hands free, so simplified slings were used. Weapons were sometimes painted with camouflage or had their shape altered with green tape.

Some RTs carried one or two 5.2lb single-shot M72 or M72A1 light antitank weapons (LAWs) for breaking contact, which fired a 66mm high-explosive anti-tank (HEAT) rocket. A LAW fired into an enemy position was quite discouraging.

Hand grenades were valuable for breaking contact and engaging the enemy closing in on the RT. The most common "frags" were the lemon-shaped M26 and the baseball-shaped M67, issued in 1967. A unique grenade used by SOG was the Dutch-made V40 fragmentation grenade. This little grenade was 1.5in. in diameter and weighed just 4.8oz. It was quite effective, could be thrown farther than the heavy US grenades, and a large number could be carried.

The M34 WP grenade was very valuable for breaking contact. Burning gobs of WP showering down on a pursuing enemy were terrifying, could begin fires to block the enemy, and generated dense smoke. The problem was that they were heavy at 1.5lb and they were difficult to throw any considerable distance. The grenade's burst threw burning particles up to 30yds, farther than the grenade could be thrown through brush.

The Colt 5.56mm XM177E1 submachine gun, also known as the Commando or CAR-15, with its butt retracted and a 20-round magazine beside it. The XM177E1 had a 10in. barrel while the XM177E2 had an 11.5in. barrel and could be fitted with a 40mm XM149 grenade launcher. The longer barrel reduced muzzle flash. (National Infantry Museum)

AN-M8 white-smoke grenades generated dense grayish-white smoke suitable for screening. The M18 colored-smoke grenades were used to mark the RT's location to aircraft and could also be used for screening. Violet and yellow "smokes" were mainly used for marking, owing to their sharp contrast with vegetation. Red smoke served to signal that an RT was in contact or to warn off a helicopter approaching a hot PZ. Green was seldom used, because it did not stand out against the lush vegetation. The NVA also had grenades of these colors, but not violet, so violet smoke was preferred for marking.

M7A2 and A3 riot-control grenades were also used to break contact, creating a cloud of tear gas for 15–35 seconds. The enemy seldom had gas masks. Besides burning the eyes, nose and throat, and temporarily blinding its victim, it caused a burning sensation in moist areas such as the underarms and groin. Many Vietnamese feared tear gas, believing that it caused sickness.

The M18A1 Claymore antipersonnel mine was a 3.5lb directional mine with 1.5lb of C4 behind 704 ball bearings, making them devastating to assaulting troops and those in ambush kill zones. It was electrically detonated by command, or it could be rigged with a tripwire. When detonated, the ball bearings blasted out in a 60-degree fan with an optimum range of 50yds, but they were dangerous up to 250yds. Blast and secondary fragmentation were dangerous within 100yds. They were set to cover approaches to RONs and they were also left on an RT's trail with a time-delay fuse if being pursued. Claymores were also used in ambushes and prisoner snatches to wipe out the bulk of the ambushed patrol.

From 1967 onwards, SOG obtained a small number of 40mm XM148 under-barrel grenade launchers, here mounted on an M16A1 rifle. They could also be fitted on the XM177E2 submachine gun, but not earlier versions. The XM148 and the improved XM203 available the following year allowed the grenadier to carry a shoulder arm easily. Note that this One-Zero is wearing a grenadier's vest, carrying 22 40mm rounds. (James Bolen via Steve Sherman)

RT West Virginia of CCN with two Americans – One-Zero Ron Knight (back row, center) and One-One Larry Kramer (front row, right) – with ten indigenous men; all are outfitted as NVA. Their armament includes Chinese 7.62mm Type 56 (AKM) assault rifles, a 40mm M79 grenade launcher (back row, second from left), and the One-One with a cut-down 7.62mm RPD machine gun. In the background is an indigenous soldier with an M79 grenade launcher. (Ron Knight via John Plaster)

A display of enemy weapons captured on missions. Against the wall, from left to right, are: four 7.62mm Type 53 (M1944) carbines, two 7.62mm SG-43 machine guns, and a 12.7mm DShKM 1938/46 machine gun. At the front are a 7.62mm RPD light machine gun to the left and a 7.62mm DP light machine gun to the right. (James Bolen via Steve Sherman)

Another pursuit-deterrence device, also set on enemy trails for harassment, was the M14 antipersonnel mine. The little "toe-popper mine" weighed only 3.5oz. Except for the firing pin it was made entirely of plastic, making it undetectable by mine detectors. It measured 56mm in diameter and was 40mm high. The 1oz shaped charge could take off a foot. They were usually buried on a trail in a diamond pattern, improving the chances of an enemy treading on one.

CONDITIONS OF SERVICE

The most common mission conducted by RTs was area recon, in which they entered a specific area to reconnoiter for enemy activity, roads and trails, facilities, etc. It was not uncommon for an area to be a "dry hole," devoid of enemy. Regardless, the RT would usually remain for its planned mission duration. They might find documents, abandoned equipment, and supplies, and be able to estimate the strength of units that had been there.

Point recon missions sent RTs to a specific grid coordinate to determine or verify what was there. It might be a suspected bridge, truck parking area, or where a radio-direction finder had located a transmitter. Road watches saw RTs attempting to creep in close enough to place a road, trail, or river under surveillance. This was extremely dangerous and seldom accomplished owing to the heavily patrolled cordon up to half a mile from these routes. Road-watch teams sometimes managed to lay antitank mines in mud holes and fords. These two missions might result in B-52 Arclight and AC-130A Spectra gunship strikes.

Bomb damage assessment (BDA) missions were hazardous as RTs were typically inserted into the impact area immediately after an Arclight strike. Almost half the B-52 strikes blasted empty jungle, with BDA teams finding either nothing, or, worse, hundreds of enemy emerging from bunkers. The RT might have to fight its way out.

Sensor and beacon missions saw teams emplacing sensors to detect foot or vehicle movement and transmit a signal. Radar-bombing beacons were emplaced at precise points, which bombers guided in on and which helped them to hit their targets.

Wiretap missions required teams to locate a telephone line, which usually paralleled roads, and tap them with voice-activated recorders. The tapes were then returned for analysis. These missions were conducted from mid-1966 to late 1970, when they were replaced by an air-dropped monitoring device that only had to land near a phone line to retransmit conversations.

Prisoner-snatch missions were dangerous, as they usually involved ambushing a larger force in order to grab a prisoner, who might be wounded. It required great imagination and flexibility to pull off. From 1966 to 1970 only 44 POWs were snatched, the maximum in one year being 12. Taking a prisoner alive on any mission resulted in a week-long period of R&R for Americans and a wristwatch or monetary reward for indigenous team members.

From 1968–69 SOG inserted exploding 7.62mm and 12.7mm ammunition under Project Eldest Son. An RT on a recon mission would leave rounds along trails used by the enemy so that they appeared to have been dropped by comrades. RTs would also insert a round into the magazines of dead enemy soldiers. Boxes of tainted 82mm mortar rounds were placed in ammunition dumps.

BELIEF AND BELONGING

Soldiers volunteering for the Special Forces did not fit any stereotyped profile. Many simply wanted to serve among the best soldiers. Others wanted adventure, a challenge, to prove themselves, or to see how far they could go. Still others thought the mission was so valuable that it was worth the risks. Loners and rebels did not fit in. Teamwork was essential: whether an A-team or an RT, there was no "I" in "team." They were generally patriotic (in a mild sense) and apolitical. It should be noted that Special Forces soldiers had the highest divorce rate in the Army, owning to their long and frequent absences. It was said that you could identify a Green Beret because he has

BELOW

A portion of the Ho Chi Minh Trail in Laos, cutting through a bamboo thicket. This photograph demonstrates just how close RTs would approach the Trail. (Frank Greco via John Plaster)

BELOW RIGHT

Way stations and rest areas were built all along the Ho Chi Minh Trail, where southbound troops would rest. These "hooches" were made of bamboo and hidden in bamboo groves, making them difficult to detect at all but the closest ranges. RTs discovering these sites reported the coordinates and photographed them so analysts could determine the most effective aerial munitions with which to attack them. (John Plaster)

"a star sapphire ring, a Seiko watch, a demolition knife, sports-car keys, and divorce papers," and that "you may meet a Green Beret you don't like, but you'll never meet one that you'll forget."

There was no typical SOG recon man. They may have had a common Special Forces background, but their previous experiences in the Army and civilian life differed greatly. While across-the-border reconnaissance demanded that detection be avoided, SOG RTs could easily find themselves in a deadly engagement. SOG recon men tended to be more aggressive than other types of reconnaissance units; they did not hesitate to fight it out. Often their aggressiveness allowed them to bluff their way out of dangerous situations through sheer brashness. They fully understood how dangerous the job was. Since they carried no US identification, the North Vietnamese were within their rights to treat them as spies and saboteurs. Team members had an agreement that if they were so severely wounded that they had to be left behind, they would not be left alive.

Like other Special Forces soldiers they firmly believed in the benefits of unconventional warfare and were not as rigid in their thinking as many conventional soldiers. They were flexible and adaptable. Doctrine and manuals meant nothing. They did whatever worked and were not afraid to try something new, no matter how unconventional. It was not uncommon for recon men to keep extending their tours six months at a time.

Freedom of action was a key feature of Special Forces and SOG operations, the rule being: "Tell me what to do and I'll do it, but don't tell me how to do it." One-Zeros were allowed a great deal of latitude and control over both their team and mission. They were given a mission and then allowed to plan every aspect of it. If someone higher up was so bold as to dictate how an RT was to perform its mission, once on the ground the One-Zero would do it his own way anyway. It was an affront for anyone to tell the man on the ground

ABOVE LEFT
A recon team cautiously trudges down a footpath of the Ho Chi Minh Trail. Such paths were not used for vehicle traffic. (Charles Aycock via Steve Sherman)

ABOVE
A recon team's photograph of one of many branch trails of the Ho Chi Minh Trail. It was common practice to place a weapon or other piece of gear in the photo to provide scale, here an XM177E2 submachine gun. (Charles Aycock via Steve Sherman)

SSG John Plaster, of RT California of CCC, upon returning from a mission. He wears olive-green jungle fatigues lightly sprayed with black bands. On his web gear are M67 fragmentation grenades and he carries an XM177E2 submachine gun along with the traditional and well deserved post-mission beer. (John Plaster)

what they thought he should do. It was only he who could see the ground and vegetation, know the capabilities and limitations of his men, have a feel for their condition and state of mind, and understood better than anyone else what the immediate enemy situation was. The One-Zero was the most experienced man, regardless of rank. There were buck sergeant One-Zeros with sergeants first class under them.

The RT was the center of their world. They were not concerned with how other RTs did their business and were not interested in anything regarding echelons above them. They looked out for their comrades, both American and indigenous. They worked, fought and played hard, with the American team members usually sticking together during stand-down.

The original RTs consisted of three Americans and 9–12 indigenous men. The large teams gave them the capability to match their strength to the mission. They could organize as a small recon team, typically with two Americans and four indigenous men, a "heavy RT" of 9–12 men allowing them to fight their way out of some situations, or as a Spike team. A Spike team was intended for direct-action missions such as recovering downed airmen, ambushes, or prisoner snatches. Many One-Zeros felt that the larger teams were too difficult to hide, made too much noise, and were still too small to fight effectively. It required two choppers to insert and extract large teams. Not all of the indigenous soldiers would be employed on every mission. There were always some indigenous troops who were on leave, injured, ill, or needed a break.

In late November 1968 RT composition was changed to two Americans and six indigenous men, owing to increasing casualties and shortages of qualified personnel. Often a third American was temporarily attached as a One-Two to break in a new man, who would later be assigned as a One-One on another team. When a "heavy RT" was needed an RT would simply be reinforced from another.

G   THE RT

This eight-man RT is depicted in the normal traveling formation, a simple column. From front to rear, they are in the following order: indigenous point man wearing NVA uniform and armed with an AKM, indigenous grenadier armed with an M79, a US One-Zero armed with an XM177E2, a US One-One with radio and armed with an XM177E2, an indigenous interpreter armed with an XM177E2, an indigenous team leader armed with a XM177E2, an indigenous grenadier armed with an M79, and an indigenous rearguard armed with an XM177E2. The rearguard wears an NVA shirt, but has a US weapon and web gear. Each man had an assigned sector of observation. They were trained to move their weapon in unison with their eyes to give them as much edge as possible if the enemy was detected at close range. Movement was extremely slow. A single step would be taken, and then each man would scan his sector closely and listen for any suspicious sounds before taking another step.

Regardless of the hazards of their mission and their hard-acquired skills and expertise, SOG recon men received no more pay than any other Special Forces soldier in Vietnam, and promotions were just as slow. SOG was generous with valor decorations, although where the act occurred was classified. They were also permitted limitless visits to in-country R&R centers during stand-down; most ordinary soldiers were typically granted just one visit.

Recon men could "un-volunteer" at anytime without criticism if they were burned out or felt that their luck had run out. If one's mindset wasn't right it was better to leave recon work. They might go to the command-and-control staff, training, Hatchet Force, or a security company. There were some recon men who felt they were indestructible, owing to good fortune and skill, but many others understood that each successful mission brought them closer to the brink.

The FOBs from which the RTs operated were self-contained compounds with barracks for the USSF and indigenous personnel, latrines, washrooms, mess halls, supply rooms, headquarters, and O&I centers. They were surrounded by defensive berms, trenches, machine-gun bunkers, and barbed-wire barriers. RT personnel typically lived in two-man rooms while the indigenous men had their own team house and quarters. There would be a modest club and dayroom with a TV showing the Armed Forces Television Network and where movies were shown.

The relations between the Americans and the indigenous men varied. First there was the language barrier. Americans had only a basic understanding of Vietnamese and the various Montagnard and other ethnic dialects were difficult. Among the indigenous team members was a designated combat interpreter, who might also be the senior indigenous man, acting as their leader and representative. It was through him that the Americans dealt with the indigenous men. Many of them spoke some basic English and most strived to learn more. This negated the Americans' opportunity to learn their language.

The indigenous members of the Special Commando Unit could be Montagnards, Cambodians, ethnic Chinese Nùngs, or Vietnamese. They were always of the same ethnicity within an RT. They knew one another well and recruited friends, relatives, or fellow villagers or tribesmen they trusted. The Americans spent some off-duty time fraternizing with their indigenous team members, but cultural differences limited this, with some spending more time with them than others. Their backgrounds, interests, and outlook differed greatly. Nonetheless, the Americans took care of their indigenous comrades on and off duty. They tried to get them the best weapons and equipment. They saw to their training and made sure that their living conditions and chow were adequate. They had to trust one another's skills and competence – their lives depended on it. The reality was that the Americans were *the* recon men. It was they who planned and prepared for the mission. They collected the intelligence information, recorded the data, made communications, and led the mission. The indigenous men were basically bodyguards to provide the necessary firepower if it came to a fight. For this they were well paid and cared for.

They were basically civilian employees of the US Government and were officially referred to as Special Commando Unit personnel, but this term was seldom used. Many had no prior military service although some had been in the CIDG camp strike forces or MIKE Forces. They were eligible for US valor awards and the Purple Heart, but it was seldom that they received anything above a Bronze Star.

RT Montana of CCN demonstrates a fully manned team with three Americans and nine indigenous Special Commando Unit Montagnards. All are armed with XM177E2 submachine guns with 30-round magazines except one man with a 7.62mm M60 machine gun. Two indigenous men possess 40mm XM149 grenade launchers. Note the One-Zero, Mike Sheppard (back center), with a .45-cal. M1911A1 pistol tucked into his STABO harness. This team had made a rare freefall parachute jump into Laos. (Billy Greenwood via John Plaster)

ON CAMPAIGN

CCN, CCC, and CCS operated independently, with overlapping areas of operation. CCN at Da Nang was the largest, and conducted operations in southern Laos and northern Cambodia. It operated FOB 1 at Phu Pai, FOB 3 at Khe Sanh (closed in mid-1968), and FOB 4 at Da Nang. CCC at Kontum operated FOB 2 from that location. It operated in the same areas as CCN. CCS was the smallest of the commands and operated out of Ban Me Thout. It was responsible for southern Cambodia.

Hatchet platoons of five USSF and 42 indigenous men served as reaction forces to exploit targets found by RTs, as well as recovery forces to aid in the extraction of RTs. Three platoons comprised an exploitation company, with at least one at each FOB. CCN and CCC possessed three or four Search, Location, and Annihilation Mission (SLAM) companies intended as reaction forces or to conduct short-term road cuts inside Laos. Each FOB also possessed a security company.

Each command possessed a reconnaissance company to which the RTs were assigned. CCN had about 30 RTs, CCC about 25, and CCS only 16. CCN and CCC RTs were named after states, and when those ran out CCN named RTs after poisonous snakes. CCS RTs were named after weapons, tools, and weather phenomena.

Mission preparation

When an RT was alerted for a mission the American members attended a briefing by the intelligence section, usually three or four days prior to insertion. Emergency missions might only allow a few hours' notice. This briefing took about an hour and specified the AO, the mission, what it was expected to achieve, enemy activity, means of insertion, date and time, and mission duration (this was flexible). The Americans planned the mission after studying maps and aerial photographs. They might discuss the AO with other teams who had been there. The One-Zero and sometimes the One-One might be flown over the AO in a forward-air-controller (FAC) aircraft known as a "Covey." He would study the terrain and select LZs and PZs as well as study his initial route.

In the remaining days the plan would be refined and changed as additional information came in. Although the team's other Americans provided input, the One-Zero's decision was final. He decided every aspect, including selecting the LZ and weapons and equipment, each man's role, the team's routes on the ground, and their PZ. The RT conducted movement and IAD rehearsals (including live-fire exercises) and trained on unique mission aspects. They also drew equipment, supplies, and fresh ammunition. Weapons were disassembled, cleaned, test fired, and then recleaned without disassembly. Radios and other electronic communications gear was tested. The radio operator received the mission frequencies, call signs, and codes.

Everyone was packed and ready by the evening before insertion. The One-Zero closely inspected each man, ensuring he had each and every item of equipment and his weapons, that he was camouflaged and made no noise when moving, that he understood all aspects of the mission, and to check on his attitude. Every man had to know who carried what critical items and where to find them. The team presented a briefback to the sergeant major or an operations officer, laying out every aspect of the mission. Questions were asked and answers provided. One of the main goals of the briefback was to check the RT's state of mind.

Besides the established FOBs, the RTs were inserted from temporary launch sites, usually Special Forces camps. Some teams were flown by C-130s to Thailand and would launch from there. An RT might spend hours or even weeks at a launch site awaiting the order to go.

RTs did most of their movement in daylight. Night movement was far too slow and noisy, and the risk of running into the enemy was high, as there were many in the vicinity of the Ho Chi Minh Trail.

Air Force North American Aviation Rockwell OV-10 Bronco FAC aircraft were used from 1969. They were armed with four 7.62mm M60 machine guns and two seven-tube 2.75in. WP rocket pods. These aircraft were painted light gray. (Frank Greco via John Plaster)

EXPERIENCE OF BATTLE

The action described in this chapter is based on a real-life operation, but has been compressed and altered for the purposes of this book. The mission called for a six-man RT to reconnoiter a small north–south valley, through which ran a little-used road. The area was heavily forested with moderate-to-dense underbrush. Air reconnaissance of roads farther to the west indicated that they were seeing less use and that this eastern road might now be seeing more traffic. The RT was to confirm or deny the road's use, assess its condition, and determine its grid coordinates on three points in order to allow it to be plotted and targeted for air attack. It was hoped that this could be accomplished in four days, but the team was prepared for a five-day stay. They were "crossing the fence" into Cambodia.

No two missions were alike and none was routine. A final readiness inspection was conducted in the operations building and the RT applied their camouflage. They walked to the helicopter pad, where the sergeant major and other staff were present. The insertion chopper arrived and the team boarded it. Each man knew exactly what he was supposed to do, the order of disembarkation, and the direction in which they were moving out.

Prior to 1970, most SOG helicopter support was provided on an as-available basis by conventional Army and Marine aviation units. SOG typically required some 45 helicopters a day for all three command-and-control operations. By the time they had learned the nuances of these special cross-border operations the units had often been changed. There were three dedicated helicopter units: the Vietnamese Air Force's 219 Helicopter

A recon team loaded and ready for insertion inside a UH-1H helicopter. In the early days, before XM177E2 submachine guns were available, RTs carried .30-cal. M2 carbines. While a US-made weapon, they were so widely available throughout Southeast Asia that they could not be attributed directly to the US. Note that a poncho is wrapped around the 7.62mm M60D door gun to protect it from dust during landing and takeoff. It would be removed when the team made their insertion run. (Warren Calkin via Steve Sherman)

Squadron with Sikorsky CH-34 Choctaws, the US Air Force's 20th Special Operations Squadron with Bell UH-1F and UH-1P (gunship) Hueys, known as the "Green Hornets," and the 21st SOS "Pony Express" Sikorsky CH-3B Sea Kings working out of Thailand.

Insertions were extremely dangerous. LZs were scarce in many areas and the NVA/VC placed lookouts on as many as possible. This was especially true in southern Laos. They might fire signal shots or dispatch a runner to alert their headquarters. To counter this, very small clearings and those overgrown with brush and saplings ("hover holes") were used, as were bomb-blasted areas.

Besides touching down on the ground, choppers would hover over inadequate LZs with the recon men hanging from the skids and dropping through the brush, rappelling from two ropes on each side, or descending a 30ft roll-out ladder on each side. Four men could rappel to the ground in five seconds, but the following men required almost a minute to hook up. An RT could descend using ladders in less than a minute, and they came into increasingly wider use.

Occasionally, false insertions were made, where a series of multiple landings were made throughout an area, with the RT being inserted at only one of these. The enemy would either attempt to dispatch patrols to all of the LZs, and being made in dim light it would be impossible to tell exactly where the touchdowns were made, or ignore some and simply be on the alert for an RT prowling the area. False insertions were seldom practiced as it overexposed helicopters to ambush. Sometimes an RT was extracted and another inserted in order to dupe the enemy.

The One-Zero would select the team's insertion time. Many preferred first light as it gave them the visibility needed to move quickly from the LZ area and then all day to move to their AO. Others preferred last light as it made it difficult for the enemy to move to and locate the LZ and find a trail. LZs were so extensively watched in Laos that CCN usually preferred insertion at last light.

Besides the insertion chopper there was a command-and-control aircraft with the launch-site CO or XO, one or two gunships (used only if the RT was engaged after insertion), and a Covey ready to call in fighter-bombers, if this was permitted.

The Vietnamese Air Force's 219th Helicopter Squadron was assigned to MACV-SOG for cross-border operations. This excellent unit was equipped with Sikorsky CH-34 Choctaw cargo helicopters. It was armed with a single .30-cal. M1919A4 machine gun in the left door. While obsolescent, the CH-34 proved reliable and effective for its mission. Kingbees were painted in a two-tone olive-green and olive-drab pattern with a light-gray underside. (John Plaster)

The insertion chopper would go in low and fast, as a low altitude reduced the chance of visual detection. It was difficult for the enemy to tell the direction of flight, especially if the chopper made S-turns on the approach. Distance was impossible to determine as there was so much sound distortion among the ridges and forest. The door gunners would be alert and the team locked and loaded. The "pucker factor" was high. The RT knew not to fire from within the aircraft, because if they did so they could hit the aircraft or the disembarking team members. The first man out was the One-Zero, and everyone followed no matter what, even if the wood line bristled with gunfire. If a two-door helicopter the One-One went out the side opposite that of the One-Zero. The chopper might not even set down. Three or four men would be in each door of a Huey.

Our particular RT hit the ground running and bee-lined into the trees; the chopper was gone before they reached them. After some 100yds they halted, accounted for everyone, ensured that nothing had been dropped, oriented the map, listened for enemy activity, and then moved out heading west-northwest. The chopper orbited some distance away as long as fuel allowed, around 10–20 minutes, and maintained radio contact with the RT. If the team

A recon team conducts training using an early type of ladder to board a hovering UH-1H helicopter. This type of narrow ladder proved to be more difficult to climb and descend than the wider ladder introduced later. (Warren Calkin via Steve Sherman)

made contact they would call for extraction from their LZ or head for a PZ. There were some instances when RTs were immediately extracted and then reinserted on an alternate LZ. The RT moved away from the LZ rapidly, but after a halt slowed to their normal movement rate. An FAC remained in the area until dark.

Movement was agonizingly slow when the enemy was in the vicinity, even when believed to be some distance away. Each man had his own surveillance sector. The point man looked for nearby threats, be it the enemy, tripwires, or natural or manmade obstacles. The man behind him looked farther forward and across a wider front for more distant threats, and kept the point man on course. The others observed to the flanks. The rearguard brought up the rear, walking backwards much of the time, or at least frequently looking over his shoulders. An RT might cover only 500–1,000yds a day in particularly dangerous areas. To move, a man meticulously scanned his sector, moving his weapon in sync with his eyes and scanning any suspicious area. He would then check the ground where he would step next, check his sector again, and move his foot. He would set it down toe first followed by his heel. The slightest crackle of dry leaves, twigs, or gravel would cause him to freeze and reposition his foot. After scanning his sector and listening he would repeat the process. They would minimize bending or breaking vegetation. The rearguard would attempt to disguise disturbed ground or bent vegetation, though there really was not much that could be done. Sweeping with a leafy branch did nothing to cover tracks, but simply looked like someone had swept the ground with a leafy branch. It was impossible to prevent tracks on muddy ground. Efforts

A door gunner readies his M60D as his UH-1H lifts off after inserting an RT. His would be the last friendly face they would see for some days. (Author's collection)

would be made to minimize scuffing the sides of gullies and stream banks or leaving marks crossing over fallen trees. There were times when men had to crouch when moving through low vegetation or even crawl on their hands and knees. This was wearing, especially crouching with full equipment. A rest halt was made every hour to drink, apply camouflage, check equipment, and listen.

RTs made three scheduled daily reports. They were made during a routine halt at no set time. This made it more difficult for the enemy to monitor calls than if they were made at set times. The first would be made around first light before the team began moving. Another was made at midday and the last at night when the team halted. The One-Zero told the radio operator what to send and he encrypted the SITREP, a relatively slow process unless the message was short. The antenna was unfolded, contact made with a Hillsboro, Moonbeam, or Covey aircraft, and the whispered message transmitted. The RT would then move out immediately.

Our team had been inserted on the east side of a ridge and the first day saw them making their way down its western side and across a stream. They crossed the stream, avoiding scuffing the bank. Once hidden on the other side, one man returned and filled all empty canteens. Shortly after leaving the stream they heard a signal shot to the south. No doubt their insertion helicopter had been seen and the shot was an effort to drive them north into a patrol. Instead, they moved southwest toward the shot while working their way up the ridge. Because their presence was now known, movement had to be extremely slow. They later heard another shot, closer this time. They had moved 700yds and it was approaching dusk. The One-Zero decided that the enemy suspected they were in this valley. Arm and hand signals were used along with the lowest whispers if speech was necessary.

Rather than RON on this side of the ridge they increased their pace and crossed to the other side. This was dangerous, as it involved moving faster and crossing the ridge crest, a natural travel avenue. They approached the crest cautiously, as the foliage was lighter there. There was no sense in watching to see if it was traveled; it either was or it wasn't. Waiting might only have them run into a patrol. They found a footpath with recent tracks. It was narrow enough for them to step across without leaving boot prints. Forming up parallel to the trail, they quickly moved across as an entity and fell into line to move rapidly downhill.

Below the crest they changed direction, heading west, then southwest and northwest. This side of the ridge was a long gradual slope down to the suspected road. Estimating that they were a quarter of the way down, and finding the brush dense, the One-Zero selected a RON. They coiled up in the densest and smallest patch they could find. The One-Zero bedded down, facing in the direction of the target road, which was designated as 12 o'clock. If they had to make a break for it they would travel at 5 o'clock to a PZ

The One-Zero to the left carries an XM148 grenade launcher on an M16A1 rifle. Note the two "mini smoke" colored-smoke grenades taped to his suspender's right shoulder strap. The XM148 proved to be flawed: it was difficult to cock, had poor sights, and its key parts easily broke. (James Bolen via Steve Sherman)

farther north on the ridge they had been inserted on. Six Claymores were emplaced and the evening SITREP was made after contacting Moonbeam. Weapons and equipment were checked, socks changed (removing one boot at a time), and the first meal of the day eaten, which consisted of cold rice and mackerel. The two Americans whispered the next day's plan and the interpreter passed it to the indigenous men. Working clockwise around their circle they each took a one-hour watch, beginning with the One-Zero. If a man snored he was nudged awake.

At 2020hrs they made out the faint sound of truck engines. Small convoys were passing on the road at irregular intervals. They estimated a total of 6–10 trucks in each of the six convoys. The One-Zero recorded the time for each, the last being at 0210hrs.

An hour before first light the team was alert. The morning SITREP was passed and breakfast eaten (rice and dried shrimp and candied pineapple chunks). They were alert for movement and sounds as dawn filtered through the trees. They recovered the Claymores and continued to listen. Just as they were moving out, three shots cracked in sequence atop the ridge, some distance apart. The RT was concerned about the possibility of an enemy sweep coming down the ridge, as well as security and patrols along the road. They had confirmed that the road was in use, but they still needed to determine its location.

The team slowly emerged from its thicket and moved downhill. The point man spotted an NVA patrol at 2 o'clock. Slowly crouching, they were stone silent as the four men passed 50yds ahead of them. After several long minutes the team moved forward. The One-Zero determined that they were on a ridge finger identifiable on the map. At its base a narrow stream curved around it and flowed down the valley. Heading down the draw on one side of the finger they approached the stream and entered its bordering brush and reeds. Carefully crossing the stream and passing through a band of brush they found the single-lane, hard-packed road. Pulling back into the brush the One-Zero worked out a six-digit coordinate based on the location of the ridge finger. They pushed on another 200yds and plotted another coordinate. The road appeared to follow the stream. That was good enough location fixing for the One-Zero. They recrossed the stream and heard two NVA soldiers walking their bicycles down the road. The interpreter reported that they were complaining about increased guard-duty hours – information of intelligence value. The RT moved back up the ridge and another patrol, of six men, passed behind them. Later, two signal shots were heard atop the ridge. Coiling up in a thicket the One-One encrypted a message confirming truck traffic, the size and interval of the convoys, and the road's coordinates. It was transmitted to Hillsboro and they requested an extraction bird to be on standby and gave the plotted PZ coordinates.

Without warning, AKs blasted through the brush from 4 o'clock, just 30yds away. The team instantly turned five XM177E2s and an M79 on the enemy. They withdrew in a peel-back IAD, throwing fragmentation and WP grenades. The One-Zero directed where they should take position and repeated the maneuver as the NVA came at them. This time they drastically veered uphill at a run. The One-One set up a Claymore with a one-minute delay and on they ran. The Claymore detonated with an echoing explosion. There was no further pursuit. They had breathing room to contact a Covey and request immediate extraction. A former One-Zero in the Covey was on the radio. Heading up the ridge they had almost gained the crest when AKs rattled from 9 o'clock. There were only two or three enemy and again grenades were thrown.

One of the indigenous men bounced into a tree and onto the ground. The team built a perimeter around him as the One-Zero tried to find the wound. The One-One started a saline IV but shortly afterwards they realized that he was dead. They had no choice but to leave the body. Another indigenous team member ripped open the man's rucksack and armed a Claymore. Others passed his magazines out and one took his XM177E2. More AKs joined the barrage and the team moved out, throwing only a few grenades as they needed to conserve them. The One-Zero ordered the team to run and then trot as they looped right, paralleling their route, before halting. Everyone loaded full magazines. The claymore detonated behind them. They soon heard the pursuing enemy to their right and to the front. Now the team stalked, veering in on the enemy from the flank. They saw seven NVA soldiers creeping low, and the RT slowly went flat. Surprise was complete when they opened fire at 20yds, emptying two magazines each.

Now they moved back uphill, cutting farther to their left. Distant shouts could be heard. Near the ridge crest they came upon very thick brush and coiled into a wagon-wheel formation. They gulped water and gave a magazine and grenade count. Fragmentation grenades were running low and there were no more WP grenades. The Covey was talking to them; extraction was 20 minutes out. That was a long time. More shouts were heard downhill. The RT moved through the thicket closer to the crest. The Covey called, "Ladders or strings?" "Ladders," came the reply. Two NVA soldiers came trotting down the crest path. The One-Zero had to order everyone to hold fire. They needed time and did not want to attract attention. The Covey came over high and reported a clearing of sorts less than 100yds down the ridge. The team moved, paralleling the crest of the ridge. The Covey came around again. "Hey good buddy, 10–15 dinks coming at you, 200yds south on the ridge trail. We got 'em." The Covey came in behind the NVA and fired two WP rockets. The RT could hear screams. The enemy knew that WP rockets marked targets for fighter-bombers. Movement on the ridge ceased for a time.

The Douglas A-1H Skyraider attack aircraft, known as a "Sandy," was valuable for close air support of RTs in trouble or to hit targets of opportunity discovered by RTs. Skyraiders carried a variety of general-purpose explosive, cluster, WP, and napalm bombs, plus 2.75in. rockets and four 20mm cannon, allowing them to attack a wide range of targets. Skyraiders were flown by the 1st, 6th, 22nd, and 602nd Special Operations Squadrons. (John Plaster)

"Five minutes out," reported the Covey. The team bee-lined for the PZ. The gunships arrived first, buzzing the ridge. AKs popped in the distance and a machine gun crackled. The One-Zero ordered the RT to reverse their hats in order to reveal the orange-lined inside. He flashed a signal mirror at the Covey. Another WP rocket struck 100yds south of them. The Covey would be using that as a reference point to give the gunships the team's location.

The enemy knew that an extraction was under way and their officers would be pressing their men to close in. They would be rewarded for destroying the team. There was movement down the ridge. The RT held its fire and set up their remaining Claymores around them. Smoke grenades were held ready to mark the PZ. The command-and-control chopper was up high. They knew urgent coordination was going on between the Covey, gunships, and the extraction bird.

The Covey came over the radio: "You're too far from the PZ. The bird's inbound." AKs suddenly rattled from below and a whistle shrieked. The team returned fire. "Blow the Claymores!" shouted the One-Zero. They all detonated with shattering blasts. "*Di di mau*!" shouted the One-Zero, urging

H **ENGAGED**

A worst-case scenario was for an RT to be engaged and suffer a serious casualty straight off, while still distant from an extraction PZ. Here, an indigenous team member has taken bullet hits in his legs. There is hope he can be saved if an extraction chopper makes it in time and the team can get him hooked up for a "string" extraction via a STABO harness, a McGuire rig, or possibly hook him to an extraction ladder, any of which could be lowered through trees if they were not too dense. The RT needed to be able to hold off the enemy for an hour. To do this they needed to undertake moves to evade them and keep them guessing about the RT's intent and destination. Ideally, they would lose their pursuers and then be able to hide out at a suitable extraction point. The main technique to losing the pursuers was to make it as difficult and dangerous for them as possible to pursue the RT, giving them an excuse to quit or at least to slow them down by forcing them to be extremely cautious. Here, the One-One prepares an M18A1 Claymore mine, which will be left on the RT's trail and timed to detonate after a one-minute delay. He is inserting the time-delay fuse fitted with an M7 blasting cap and an M60 fuse igniter. The One-Zero is treating the wounded team member. Teams could not carry blood plasma, but they might carry serum albumin contained in a key-and-strip-opened can. This was a blood-volume expander that absorbed bodily fluids into the circulatory system to prevent its collapse from loss of blood. Ideally a 500ml bag of saline solution would be administered through an intravenous injection in order to provide additional fluid. The serum-albumin can contained a 100ml bottle of serum albumin, a plastic bag-like suspension sling, an airway cannula (a needle inserted into the bottle's stopper to let in air, aiding the albumin flow), and the injection needle and rubber tube.

An RT rapidly boards a Huey on a PZ deep in Laos. The number of men that could load into a Huey often determined the RT's size. Trying to get a second chopper into a PZ to take out the second part of an RT when it was under pursuit could be disastrous. (Mike Sloniker via John Plaster)

his men to move quickly. Throwing grenades as they went, the team darted toward the PZ. It was not much of one, being covered in thin brush and saplings, but it was clear enough for a ladder extraction. They pulled their STABO harness leg straps down and connected them.

They could hear the chopper. Violet smoke was tossed. AKs cracked and whistled. The chopper came in at treetop level, with the 35ft ladders unrolling. The door gunners were hammering their M60 machine guns into the trees. Team members were spraying fire, emptying their magazines. Dust and leaves billowed from the rotor blast, blinding both the RT and the enemy. Two men leapt onto each ladder, with the One-Zero grabbing on last, after throwing his final grenade. They didn't try to climb in, but hooked onto the ladders with their STABO harness snap links. Bullets whizzed past them as they lifted off and the gunships rolled in, giving the ridge a good pasting with rockets and guns. Clinging to the ladders, it was a long ride back to the FOB skimming over the treetops.

CCC One-Zeros formed up with the Zero-Twos and their indigenous teams lined up behind them. They are waiting to greet a returning RT. (Ted Wilcorek via John Plaster)

Post-mission

En route to the FOB the RT might sit down on a friendly airstrip and climb inside the helicopter. If the extraction had been particularly hairy then everyone who was free at the FOB would turn out to greet the returning patrol. If things had gone according to plan then the launch officer and a few buddies would be on hand. The RT members would stow their gear and get the indigenous men started on equipment and weapons maintenance. The Americans would buy beers or soft drinks at the small FOB clubhouse and then report to the "S-2 hole." An officer and an NCO conducted the debriefing. The One-Zero talked through every aspect of the mission, in virtually a minute-by-minute narrative. Specific questions regarding intelligence information were asked. A shorter hand-written narrative on a pre-printed form would also be completed, the RT's track of its movement rendered on a map, any map updates plotted, and lessons learned of value to other RTs discussed.

RT members relax outside their mess hall after returning from a mission. They wear standard US olive-green jungle fatigues and a variety of boonie hats. (James Bolen via Steve Sherman)

RTs were given at least 3–4 days' stand-down time after a mission. A week off was given if possible before the team went back into cycle ready to be assigned a mission. In the meantime they trained, conducted weapons firing, implemented lessons learned, and practiced techniques.

AFTERMATH OF BATTLE

MACV–SOG was deactivated on April 30, 1972. CCN, CCC, and CCS had been reorganized and reduced as Task Force 1, 2, and 3 Advisory Elements, respectively, in March 1972 to assist the ARVN Special Mission Service under the Strategic Technical Directorate, which had taken over the SOG reconnaissance mission.

SOG RTs had accomplished a great deal over the years, but the cost was high. A dozen entire RTs disappeared and never made radio contact after insertion. A total of 49 US SOG members are still listed as missing in action along with scores of indigenous personnel[8]. The number of US SOG personnel killed in action was 407. Virtually 100 percent of RT members were casualties at some point, with an incredibly high number of wounded. It is said that the RTs suffered higher casualty rates than even Civil War regiments. While Special Forces personnel assigned to MACV–SOG made up only 10 percent of the Special Forces in Vietnam, they suffered over half the number of Special Forces members killed in action and 85 percent of those who went missing. There were only a few rare exceptions under unusual circumstances when RT members were taken prisoner.

Some suffered post-traumatic stress disorder owing to the continuous and intense psychological and physical stress and anxiety. Some did not experience it for many years and it manifested itself in many ways. The physical strain and various illnesses such as malaria, dysentery, and dengue fever too took their toll. The areas the RTs operated in were often saturated with Agent Orange and CS (tear-gas) powder.

8 Policy was that even if a man was seen shot, confirmed dead, and left behind, he was
 considered missing in action unless the body was recovered.

With no small effort this CCS recon team was extracted with the launcher tube of a camouflage-painted Chinese-made 122mm DKB rocket launcher. There was a prevalent fear that higher headquarters would disbelieve RT reports of what they discovered and it was not uncommon for them to go to great efforts to return with a sample. (James Bolen via Steve Sherman)

General Westmoreland declared that up to 50 percent of intelligence on enemy troop locations and logistical activities received by MACV was provided by Special Forces, while SOG supplied some 75 percent of the intelligence on the Ho Chi Minh Trail. RTs are also credited with the highest enemy-to-friendly kill ratio, inclusive of directed air strikes: 158 enemy to one friendly in 1970. As many as 100,000 NVA personnel supported the Ho Chi Minh Trail and a large percentage of these were infantry, security, and counter-reconnaissance troops necessary to counter small RTs. These were troops that could have otherwise been employed on combat operations inside South Vietnam.

Eight Special Forces members assigned to SOG were awarded the Medal of Honor, along with two Navy SEALs and an Air Force special-operations officer. A total of 23 MACV–SOG members received the Distinguished Service Cross, the second-highest medal for valor, and over 2,000 other awards for valor were presented. SOG itself was finally awarded the much-deserved Presidential Unit Citation in 2001.

As an example of the valor displayed by SOG recon men, Sergeant First Class Jerry M. Shriver (CCS), MIA April 24, 1969, during his 3½ years' continuous service in Vietnam was presented with: two Silver Stars, one Soldier's Medal, seven Bronze Stars for Valor, one Air Medal, three Army Commendation Medals for Valor, and one Purple Heart.

SOG cross-border operations remained classified until the 1980s, when the files were declassified. Regardless of what some believe, SOG operations are no longer classified.